Corporate Acquisitions and Mergers in Nigeria

Corporate Acquisitions and Mergers in Nigeria

Ladi Taiwo
Alayo Ogunbiyi
Isoken Iyamu

Abdulai, Taiwo & Co.

This book was originally published as a chapter in Corporate Acquisitions and Mergers.

General Editor: Peter Begg

Wolters Kluwer

Published by:
Kluwer Law International B.V.
PO Box 316
2400 AH Alphen aan den Rijn
The Netherlands
E-mail: international-sales@wolterskluwer.com
Website: lrus.wolterskluwer.com

Sold and distributed by:
Wolters Kluwer Legal & Regulatory U.S.
7201 McKinney Circle
Frederick, MD 21704
United States of America
Email: customer.service@wolterskluwer.com

ISBN 978-94-035-3021-5

e-Book: ISBN 978-94-035-2981-3
web-PDF: ISBN 978-94-035-2982-0

Contents

Abdulai, Taiwo & Co.

Abdulai, Taiwo & Co. is a leading full-service commercial and IP law firm with a long-standing reputation for excellence. Extensively consulted on Nigerian business regulatory issues, the firm has acted in many of the most significant transactions in Nigeria's capital market, as well as in cross-border mergers, acquisitions and divestitures. The reputation of the firm's M&A, corporate/commercial practice is consistently confirmed by international rating agencies: *Chambers Global; Legal 500 (EMEA); and IFLR 1000*. *Chambers Global,* 2018 remarked that 'Abdulai, Taiwo & Co. is well respected for its considerable corporate and commercial reputation and retained by clients from a variety of sectors.' *Legal 500 (EMEA),* 2013 edition remarked that 'Abdulai, Taiwo & Co. stands out for its experience in cross-border M&A work.' IFLR 1000, 2017 also remarked that 'Abdulai, Taiwo & Co. is a well-respected member of the Nigeria legal scene, with a good offering across the spectrum of financial and corporate law.'

Authors

Ladi Taiwo, the senior partner of the firm, is the chair of the M&A, corporate/ commercial, practice. An author of several leading practice books and works on the Nigerian business regulatory environment, international rating agencies such as *Chambers Global; Legal 500 (EMEA); IFLR 1000; Who's Who Legal* has consistently ranked Ladi Taiwo as a leading lawyer in the fields of corporate/ commercial, M&A and banking. According to *IFLR: 1000,* 2020 edition: **Ladi Taiwo** has 'Excellent responsiveness, great contacts deep experience and recall, interested in his client's success.' 'Ladi is deservedly a luminary in commercial practice. His professionalism and sound expertise are stellar.' *Chambers Global* described **Ladi Taiwo** as a 'quiet but strong and reliable all-round lawyer.' *Who's Who Legal* year 2018 edition remarked that '**Ladi Taiwo** impresses peers and clients alike with the breadth of his expertise. He is frequently called upon to manage complex domestic and cross-border transactions for key clients.'

Alayo Ogunbiyi, the partner of the firm, is the chair of the Capital Markets and Corporate finance group. She is consistently recommended as a leading lawyer in her field in *Chambers Global, IFLR 1000 and Who's Who Legal. Who's Who Legal,* 2018 edition remarked that '**Alayo Ogunbiyi** is a capital markets expert who enjoys a fantastic reputation in the market for her top-tier work on structured finance matters.' *Chambers Global,* 2020 edition said, '**Alayo Ogunbiyi** is noted for her wide-ranging expertise and experience acting on the lender-side of finance transactions; project finance, bond issuances and private placement.'

Isoken Iyamu is an associate counsel of the firm. Educated at the University of Lagos, the Nigerian Law School, the Institute of Chartered Secretaries and Administrators and the Chartered Institute of Arbitrators, she has been an active member of the firm's corporate/commercial department since 2017.

Lagos (Head Office):

Goodwill House

Ikorodu Road,

P.O. Box 536, Yaba

Lagos, Nigeria

Tel.: +234 (0) - 1 2911181;

(234) 705 268 1536

E-mail: law@abdulaitaiwo.com

Website: www.abdulaitaiwo.com

Abuja:

Ndamella House (Suite A-11), 278,

Plot 500, Tafawa Balewa Way,

Area 3, Garki,

P.O. Box 2916, Abuja, Nigeria

Tel.: + 234 (0) – 9- 9502101;

1 LOCAL ECONOMIC, POLITICAL AND CULTURAL ASPECTS

1.1 Country Profile

[01] The Federal Republic of Nigeria, located in West Africa, is comprised of thirty-six States of the Federation and a Federal Capital Territory. The land boundaries to Nigeria are Benin, Cameroon, Chad and Niger. With a total land area of 923,768 square kilometres and an estimated population of over 200 million people, Nigeria is the largest market in sub-Saharan Africa with reasonably skilled potential manpower. It is estimated that 75% of its population above the age of 15 years are literate.

[02] Nigeria is a secular state, and religions practised include Christianity, Islam, and indigenous beliefs. Although there are over 250 ethnic groups with several ethnic languages and dialects, the official language for business communications is the English language. The local currency of Nigeria is the Naira (NGN).

[03] GDP real growth rate in the opening quarter of 2020 was 1.87% with the Oil sector as well as Information and Communication (Telecommunications), Financial and Insurance (Financial Institutions), Agriculture (Crop Production), Mining and Quarrying (Crude Petroleum & Natural Gas), and Construction recording the highest volume of growth.

[04] The core natural resources available in Nigeria are mineral fuels (including oil), tin, iron ore, coal, limestone, niobium, lead, zinc, and arable land where agricultural produce, such as oil palm, rubber, cassava (tapioca), sorghum and peanuts are grown for consumption and export. The following export product groups, which account for 99% of the overall value of Nigeria's global shipments, represent the highest dollar value in Nigerian global shipments in 2019:

- Mineral fuels including oil: USD 46.7 billion (87.1% of total exports)
- Ships, boats: USD 3.2 billion
- Other base metal goods: USD 2.1 billion
- Cocoa: USD 311.1 million
- Oilseeds: USD 299.7 million
- Fertilizers: USD 151.7 million
- Fruits, nuts: USD 113.4 million
- Tobacco, manufactured substitutes: USD 103.7 million
- Raw hides, skins not fur skins, leather: USD 75.3 million
- Aircraft, spacecraft: USD 69.8 million

[05] One of the key developmental challenges constraining the growth of the Nigerian economy is the huge deficit in basic infrastructure services, especially in the areas of energy and transportation. To close the yawning infrastructure gap, it was apparent that the massive road and rail investments to be made were well beyond the resources and capacity of the Government which had been solely responsible for the provision of such services. The Federal Government, therefore, recognized the imperative of leveraging on private sector investment and capacity to bridge the country's enormous infrastructure gap through an effective framework for Public Private Partnership. Consequently, the Infrastructure Concession Regulatory Commission (ICRC) was legally constituted, to provide the requisite regulatory and institutional framework within which all Ministries, Departments and Agencies of the Federal Government can effectively enter into partnership with the private sector in the financing, construction, operation and maintenance of infrastructure projects. The ICRC developed the National Policy on Public Private Partnerships (PPP) to provide clear and consistent process and procedure guides for all aspects of PPP projects development and implementation from project identification, evaluation, selection, to procurement, operation, maintenance and performance monitoring. The national PPP policy was launched in 2009, and state governments are being encouraged to embrace private finance initiatives for infrastructure developments.

[06] Other developmental challenges include corruption, crime and terrorism (specifically the Boko Haram insurgency). However, the administration of Muhammadu Buhari GCFR (current President of Nigeria) has taken steady steps to combat these challenges, such as the formulation of a whistleblowing policy under the Whistle Blowing Act, and the reforms of antiterrorism laws.

[07] The Federal Government of Nigeria established the National Social Investment Office (NSIO) within the Presidency but more specifically, the Office of the Vice President in 2016, with the goal to undertake and guarantee high-level political authority and coordination for all social protection programmes within Nigeria. These National Social Investment Programmes (NSIP) targeted at the vulnerable and unemployed citizens include Conditional Cash Transfer (CCT) Programme, National Home-Grown School Feeding Programme (NHGSFP), N-Power Programme, and the Enterprise and Empowerment Programme (GEEP). The NSIP is currently domiciled under the Federal Ministry of Humanitarian Affairs, Social Development and Disaster Management.

1.1.1 Trade and Industrial Policy

[08] Nigeria's current trade and industrial policy is anchored on a guided deregulation of the economy and the Government's disengagement from all activities which are private sector oriented, leaving the Government to play the role of facilitator, by concentrating on the provision of incentives policy, and infrastructure necessary to allow the private sector to play the role of engine of growth. The industrial policy is intended to:

- generate productive employment and raise productivity;
- increase export of locally manufactured goods;
- create a wider geographical dispersal of industries;
- improve the technological skills and capability available in the country;
- increase the local content of industrial output by looking inward for the supply of basic and intermediate inputs;

- attract direct foreign capital; and
- increase private sector participation.

[09] Among other policy objectives, the liberalization of the exchange control regime was designed to facilitate and enhance trading activities. Items on the import prohibition list are amended from time to time, with government opting to utilize tariff structures to ensure local content development, protect end-user product pricing of local industries, and discourage frivolous imports.

[10] In August 2019, the Nigerian borders were closed to imported goods in a bid to end rampant smuggling across the porous frontiers and strengthen domestic agriculture as it looks to diversify the oil-dependent economy. In 2020, the Ministry for Industry, Trade and Investment issued a statement to the effect that the borders would be reopened on the recommendation of its joint border patrol comprising of the Nigerian Customs Service and other federal security agencies, that the bordering countries had fully complied with all trade protocols laid by ECOWAS.

[11] On July 7 2019, Nigeria signed the Africa Continental Free Trade Area (AfCFTA) Agreement. The AfCFTA is a continent-wide free trade agreement brokered by the African Union (AU) that requires its members to adopt certain practices that will allow free access to commodities, goods, and services across the continent. It is intended to accelerate intra-African trade and boosting Africa's trading position in the global market by strengthening Africa's common voice and policy space in global trade negotiations. The implementation of the first phase of the AfCFTA scheduled for July 1 2020, has been stalled by the global COVID-19 pandemic.

[12] The National Economic Intelligence Committee has adopted a mission statement captioned 'Vision 20-2020', which proclaims that:

> By 2020 Nigeria will be one of the 20 largest economies in the world, able to consolidate its leadership role in Africa and establish itself as a significant player in the global economic and political arena.

[13] The overall mission objective is for Nigeria to become the emerging market destination of choice to investors. Currently, Nigeria is ranked 27th in terms of GDP size globally. However, it has one of the highest number of people living in poverty globally.

1.1.2 Government and Political System

[14] After several years of military rule ending in February 1999, Nigeria has been operating a multi-party democracy. Elections into the Federal and thirty-six State Governments are for four-year terms and have generally been peacefully conducted. Quite uncommon in Africa, the 2015 national elections saw the then incumbent President, as a candidate of the ruling party, losing the election to the candidate of an opposition and conceding electoral defeat.

[15] The capital and seat of the Federal Government are located in Abuja, Federal Capital Territory, whilst each State has its own capital. Government is statutorily guided by the Federal Constitution of May 1999, under the following branches of administration:

Executive Branch

Head of Government	– President
Cabinet	– Federal Executive Council
Elections	– President is elected by popular vote for no more than two four-year terms.

Legislative Branch

[16] The National Assembly consists of the **Senate** (109 seats, members elected by popular vote to serve four-year terms) and the **House of Representatives** (360 seats, members elected by popular vote to serve four-year terms).

Judicial Branch

[17] Supreme Court (judges appointed by the President); Federal Court of Appeal (judges appointed by Federal Government on the advice on the Judicial Advisory Committee); and the Federal High Court (Judges appointed by the Federal Government on the recommendation of the Judicial Advisory Committee).

Administrative Divisions:	Thirty-six States and the Federal Capital Territory
North-West Zone:	Jigawa, Kano, Katsina, Kebbi, Sokoto, Zamfara
North-East Zone:	Adamawa, Bauchi, Borno, Gombe, Taraba, Yobe
North-Central Zone:	Benue, Kaduna, Kogi, Kwara, Nassarawa, Niger, Plateau
South-East Zone:	Abia, Anambra, Ebonyi, Enugu, Imo
South-West Zone:	Ekiti, Lagos, Ogun, Ondo, Osun, Oyo
South-South Zone:	Akwa Ibom, Bayelsa, Cross River, Delta, Edo, Rivers

Federal Character Imperatives:

[18] As a manifestation of Nigeria's federal character, appointments to ministerial and top government positions must reflect representation from each of the thirty-six states of the federation.

1.2 Membership of Trade Alliances/ Associations and Political Groups

[19] Nigeria is a participating member of the following regional and international organizations:

The African, Caribbean and Pacific Group of States (ACP Group); African Development Bank; African Union; Economic Community of West African States (ECOWAS); Food and Agriculture Organization of the United Nations (FAO), G-15, G-24, G-77, International Atomic Energy Agency (IAEA); International Bank for Reconstruction and Development (IBRD); International Civil Aviation Organization (ICAO), International Chamber of Commerce (ICC); International Centre for Counter-Terrorism (ICCT), International Confederation of Free Trade Unions (ICFTU); ICRM, International Development Association (IDA); International Fund for Agricultural Development (IFAD); International Finance Corporation (IFC); International Federation of Red Cross and Red Crescent Societies (IFRC); International Hydrographic Organization (IHO); International Labour Organization (ILO); International Monetary Fund (IMF); International Maritime Organization (IMO); Interpol, International Olympic Committee (IOC); International Organization for Migration (IOM); International Standard Organization (ISO); International Telecommunication Union (ITU); Multilateral Investment Guarantee Agency (MIGA); Mission des Nations Unies pour l'Organisation d'un Référendum au Sahara Occidental (MINURSO); Mission de l'Organisation de Nations Unies en République Démocratique du Congo (MONUC); Non-Aligned Movement (NAM); United Nations Operation in Burundi (ONUB); Organization for the Prohibition of Chemical Weapons (OPCW); Organization of Petroleum Exporting Countries (OPEC); United Nations (UN), United Nations Mission in Sierra Leone (UNAMSIL); United Nations Conference on Trade and Development (UNCTAD); United Nations Educational, Scientific and Cultural Organization (UNESCO); United Nations High Commissioner for Refugees (UNHCR); United Nations Industrial Development Organization (UNIDO); United Nations Institute for Training and Research (UNITAR); United Nations Mission In Ethiopia Eritrea (UNMEE):United Nations Interim Administration Mission in Kosovo (UNMIK);United Nations Mission in Liberia (UNMIL); United Nations Monitoring, Verification and Inspection Commission (UNMOVIC); Universal Postal Union (UPU); World Customs Organization (WCO); World Federation of Trade Unions (WFTU); World Health Organization (WHO); World Intellectual Property Organization (WIPO); World Meteorological Organization (WMO); World Trade Organization (WTO).

1.2.1 The Legal System

[20] There is no comprehensive codified Commercial Code, as it is actually impossible to fashion out such a Code in Nigeria due to its federal structure, and the applicability of local laws to the location of commercial entities. Consequently, there are several laws which govern commercial activity in the country with the general business laws originally founded on English common law.

[21] The various laws that govern commercial activity were adopted/enacted at different times. This shows the dynamism of the system, as the law moves with the general business climate to meet needs as they arise.

[22] This is a marked difference from what obtains in all the sixteen French-speaking countries of West and Central Africa. All the countries have a uniform commercial code ('OHADA') that is harmonized with the French civil code. This clarification is deemed necessary to guide some people who erroneously assume that all the countries within the Economic Community of West African States (ECOWAS) have a common Commercial Code.

[23] Legal proceedings in Nigeria are adversarial and tailored towards the general trend in most common law jurisdictions. Companies are treated as juristic entities separate from principal officers and shareholders.

[24] The Nigerian legal system is fundamentally predicated on the hierarchy of Courts. Courts of First Instance jurisdiction in disputes involving companies are State High Court(s) or Federal High Court(s), where trials are decided by a single presiding judge. Appeals are decided at the Court of Appeal by a panel of three judges, and further appeal rests at the Supreme Court (which is the highest Court) constituted by a panel of five justices. In each forum of appeal, the litigant has no advance information on the composition of the adjudicating panel of judges/justices.

[25] Judicial precedents and the doctrine of *stare decisis* are followed, and lower courts are bound by decisions of both the Supreme Court and the Court of Appeal. The Court of Appeal is itself bound to follow and apply decisions of the Supreme Court that have not been expressly overruled.

1.2.2 Judiciary

[26] The supreme law in Nigeria is the Constitution of the Federal Republic of Nigeria (Promulgation) Act No. 24 of 1999, which has been the organic law since May 1999.

[27] Judicial decisions are independent of the executive branch and other political influences. Under the Constitution, judges are to be appointed on the recommendation of the National Judicial Council. Where the appointment is to a federal judicial office, the President makes the appointment subject to the confirmation of the Senate. Access to the Courts is easy, but court litigation is a rather protracted process in Nigeria as Judges' chambers and court filing systems are not yet computerized, which presents grave challenges for archiving and records retrieval.

1.3 Commercial Jurisdiction of Federal High Courts in Nigeria

[28] The Federal High Courts in Nigeria maintain commercial jurisdiction over the following:

(1) Matters connected with or pertaining to banking, banks and other financial institutions, but not related to disputes between an individual customer and his bank.
(2) Matters arising from the operation of the Companies and Allied Matters Act, 1990 (viz. the Companies' Law of Nigeria).
(3) Matters on admiralty jurisdiction.
(4) Matters on any federal enactment relating to trademarks, copyright, patent, designs, etc.
(5) Aviation and Safety of aircraft.
(6) Mines and Minerals (including oil fields, oil mining, and natural gas).

1.3.1 Other Jurisdiction of Federal High Courts in Nigeria

[29] Other jurisdiction of the Nigeria Federal High Courts includes:

- Matters relating to the revenue of the Government.
- Matters connected with or pertaining to the taxation of companies and other bodies established or carrying on business in Nigeria.
- Matters connected with or pertaining to customs and excise duties and export duties, etc.
- Bankruptcy and insolvency.
- Drugs and poisons.
- Weights and measures.
- Interpretation and operation of the Constitution (1999) in so far as it affects the Federal Government or any of its agencies.
- Any action or proceeding for a declaration or injunction affecting the validity of any executive or administrative action or decision by the Federal Government or any of its agencies.

[30] It is important to note that in all the aforementioned cases, the Federal High Court shall have and exercise jurisdiction to the exclusion of any other court in civil cases and matters while its jurisdiction in criminal cases and matters are concurrent with the High Courts of states.

1.4 Other Court Systems and Tribunals for Disputes of Commercial or Industrial Nature

1.4.1 National Industrial Court

[31] The National Industrial Court (NIC) was established to resolve disputes arising from or connected with any labour, employment, trade unions, industrial relations and matters arising from the workplace, the conditions of service, including health, safety, the welfare of labour, employee and worker. Appeals from the NIC go to the Court of Appeal.

1.4.2 Industrial Arbitration Panel

[32] This Panel was set up for the resolution of collective trade and industrial disputes. The Industrial Arbitration Panel (IAP) is used where a mediator/conciliator appointed by the Minister in charge of labour matters is unable to settle disputes between parties to the dispute. Where the award of the IAP is objected to by any of the parties, the matters will be referred to the National Industrial Court whose award is final and binding. This process could be an effective way of settling disputes. But in actual practice, the parties do not usually honour such agreements and often resort to industrial strikes and picketing without even resorting to the labour panels.

1.4.3 Administrative Proceedings Committee

[33] The Committee was established by *the Companies and Allied Matters Act 2020* to provide an opportunity to be heard for persons alleged to have contravened the provision of the act, resolve disputes or grievances arising from the operation of the act and impose administrative penalties for the contravention of the act. Parties aggrieved as a result of the decisions of the Committee can appeal to the court of competent jurisdiction.

1.4.4 Tax Appeal Tribunal

[34] This was set up as forum of first instance, for the resolution of all tax disputes arising from operations of the various Tax Laws such as the Companies Income Tax Act (CITA), Petroleum Profit Tax Act (PPTA), Personal Income Tax Act (PITA), Capital Gains Tax Act, Stamp Duties Act, and Value Added Tax Act. Both the taxpayer and relevant tax authority can initiate the appeal process.

[35] The tribunals are constituted for different administrative divisions of the country, and the composition of each tribunal panel include a chartered accountant, legal practitioner and tax administrator.

1.4.5 Investments and Securities Tribunal ('IST')

[36] In view of the technical nature of operations and transactions in the capital market, inadequate capacity among the judges and lawyers were causing inordinate delays in the adjudication of disputes before the regular courts. Therefore, to ensure that capital market disputes were promptly resolved and overseen by persons with relevant knowledge and experience, the IST was established as a forum of first instance for dispute relating to securities and all other matters regulated by the Securities and Exchange Commission ('SEC'), including disputes with SEC. The Investment and Securities Tribunal consists of nine persons referred to as Capital Market Assessors, one of whom shall be the Chairman of the tribunal. They are all to be appointed by the federal minister of Finance. The chairman of the tribunal is expected to be a legal practitioner qualified to practice for a period of not less than 15 years with cognate experience in capital market matters. The quorum of the tribunal is five members, and it is only a person who is knowledgeable about the laws and regulations, norms, practices and operations of the capital market that is qualified for appointment as a Capital Market Assessor for a period of five years from the date on which he assumes office. Capital Market Assessors on any constituted tribunal panel include lawyers, stockbrokers, registrars, accountants. The composition of the tribunal emphasizes both legal expertise and industry expertise.

[37] The tribunal shall, to the exclusion of any other court of law or body in Nigeria, exercise jurisdiction to adjudicate on matters relating to the following:

- the interpretation of any law, enactment or regulations to which Investment and Securities law applies;
- disputes between the Commission (SEC) and a securities exchange or Capital Trade Point;
- disputes between capital market operators and the Securities Exchange or Capital Trade Point;
- disputes between capital market operators;
- disputes between capital market operators and their clients; and
- disputes between quoted companies and the regulators or the Securities Exchanges.

[38] Any person aggrieved by any action or decision of the SEC under these laws may also institute an action or appeal any decision before the tribunal. The tribunal has rules regulating its procedures, and the tribunal has the power for the purposes of discharging its functions under the law to:

- summon and enforce the attendance of any person and examine him on oath;
- to require the discovery and production of documents,
- receive evidence on affidavits,
- call for the examination of witnesses or documents,
- review its decisions,
- dismiss an application for default or deciding matters ex parte,
- set aside any order or dismissal of any application for default or any order passed by it ex parte; or

- do anything which in the opinion of the tribunal is incidental or ancillary to its functions under the law.

1.5 Arbitration and Alternative Dispute Resolution ('ADR')

1.5.1 The Arbitration and Conciliation Act

[39] The Arbitration and Conciliation Act ('**the Arbitration Act**') was promulgated in 1988 with the declared intention of providing a unified legal framework for the fair and efficient settlement of commercial disputes by arbitration and conciliation. The Act also makes the Convention on the Recognition and Enforcement of Arbitral Awards (New York Convention) applicable to any award in Nigeria or indeed in any contracting State arising out of international commercial arbitration.

1.5.2 Some Practical Implications of the Arbitration Act on Commercial Transactions

[40] An extensive discussion on the merits and demerits of arbitration per se is beyond the scope of this work. However, it will endeavour to address some of the more common types of enquiries that could guide investors in their commercial transactions.

Q. Are there any Opportunities Available in Nigeria for Conciliation and Amicable Settlement of Disputes?

Many jurisdictions do not recognize 'conciliation' as a formal institution, in the context of private arbitration. However, it is becoming more apparent that contractual parties often consider it expedient to explore opportunities for amicable settlement of some contractual aspects of a dispute, even pending any formal arbitration proceedings. In this regard, the conciliation rules of the Nigerian Arbitration Act are quite unique in providing that: -

> Notwithstanding the other provisions of this Act, the parties to any agreement may seek amicable settlement of any dispute in relation to the agreement by *conciliation* under the provisions of this Part of the Act.

Whilst the Arbitration Act may be a local statutory enactment, in its application, it seems to have certain favourable features in respect of international contracts, where either one of the parties is based in Nigeria, or the contract between the parties is to be executed in Nigeria. For example:-

- there is a clearly stipulated opportunity for an interim conciliation procedure towards amicable settlement of disputes;

- the location of conciliation and/or arbitration proceedings could be such jurisdictions as have been mutually agreed by the parties, i.e., in Nigeria or elsewhere;
- adoption of the provisions of the Arbitration Act as the applicable arbitration rules of any international contract puts to rest any doubts as to applicable law to the contract and issue of enforceability;
- the sequence and modes of the dispute resolution opportunities offered by the Act may be less protracted and more cost-effective than some of the Convention assimilated arbitration rules and other arbitration bodies.

Q. Under The Nigerian Law, Is a 'Choice of Laws' Provision In A Contract Enforceable?

There are certain categories of contracts which must expressly designate Nigerian laws as the applicable law, e.g., contracts/agreements relating to the transfer of technology to any Nigerian entity, which attracts royalties and fees in connection with the use of trademarks, patented inventions, the supply of technical expertise, etc.; or the case of contracts/agreements for the supply of goods and/or services to Federal and State governments of Nigeria. As regards other international commercial contracts, and depending on the manner in which the agreement is couched, the parties are free under the Nigerian law to choose the applicable law to the transaction.

Section 47(1) of the Arbitration Act clearly states that:

> The arbitral tribunal shall decide the dispute in accordance with the rules in force in the country the parties have chosen as applicable to the substance of the dispute.

Q. Can there be a Mandatory Arbitration Agreement Whereby the Parties, Rather than Resorting to the Court System, Utilize Formal Arbitration Proceedings?

'Yes', there can be a mandatory Arbitration Agreement between the parties. However, such an agreement must be clearly incorporated in the contract between the parties with specific clauses prescribing the following:

- the applicable law;
- the language of construction agreed by the parties;
- the arbitration procedures applicable, and that the parties shall regard the arbitral awards as final;
- the place where the parties have agreed to hold the arbitral proceedings.

Q. What Arbitration Organization Would Be Most Suitable or Recognized in Nigeria?

According to the Act, the parties to an international commercial agreement may agree in writing that disputes in relation to the agreement shall be referred to arbitration in accordance with the Arbitration Rules set out in the Arbitration and Conciliation Act of Nigeria, or the UNCITRAL Arbitration Rules or any other international arbitration rules acceptable to the parties. Whilst the parties are at liberty to choose such international arbitration rules as they deem fit, it would be quite reasonable to propose the adoption of the UNCITRAL Arbitration Rules (as set out by the United Nations Commission on International Trade Law on 21 June 1985); more so, as it is the only arbitration organization specifically incorporated and acknowledged by reference within the Arbitration and Conciliation Act of Nigeria. Reciprocal enforcement of arbitral awards is also assured since Nigeria has ratified and is a party to the '**Convention on the Recognition and Enforcement of Foreign Arbitral Awards**' concluded at New York on 10 June 1958.

Q. What Are the Limits of Court Intervention in Nigeria to Arbitration Agreements?

By virtue of Section 2 of the Arbitration Act, an unequivocally expressed 'arbitration agreement shall be irrevocable except by agreement of the parties or by leave of the Court or a judge.' In this connection, the law prescribes that 'a Court before which an action which is the subject of an arbitration agreement is brought shall, if any party so requests ...... order a stay of proceedings and refer the parties to arbitration.' In other words, the courts in Nigeria would ordinarily not interfere where the parties themselves have voluntarily elected to resolve their disputes by way of arbitration. In fact, an arbitral award, irrespective of the country in which it is made, is recognized as binding and would be enforced upon application in writing to a court by one of the parties.

[41] From the foregoing, it seems obvious that the Nigerian courts are still seised of residuary or 'last resort' jurisdiction. Having stated this, one area of potential difficulty must be pointed out. Section 54(1) of the Act seems to convey the impression that arbitral awards in Convention countries may be enforced as final in their application to differences arising out of legal relationships which are contractual whereas Section 32 of the Arbitration Act, provides that:

> Any of the parties to an arbitration may request the court to refuse recognition or enforcement of the awards.

Amongst the circumstances stipulated for the setting aside of an arbitral award by a Nigerian court are instances where the party making the application furnishes proof:

(i) 'that a party to the arbitration agreement was under some incapacity;
(ii) that the arbitration agreement is not valid under the law which the parties have indicated should be applied, or failing such indication, that the arbitration agreement is not valid under the laws of Nigeria;

(iii) that he was not given proper notice of the appointment of an arbitrator or of the arbitral proceedings or was otherwise not able to present his case, or
(iv) that the award deals with a dispute not contemplated by or not falling within the terms of the submission to arbitration, or
(v) that the award contains decisions on matters which are beyond the scope of the submission to arbitration, so however that if the decisions on matters submitted to arbitration can be separated from those not submitted, only that part of the award which contains decisions on matters not submitted to arbitration may be set aside, or
(vi) that the composition of the arbitral tribunal, or the arbitral procedure, was not in accordance with the agreement of the parties, unless such agreement was in conflict with a provision of this Act from which the parties cannot derogate, or
(vii) where there is no agreement between the parties under sub-paragraph (vi) of this paragraph, that the composition of the arbitral tribunal or the arbitral procedure was not in accordance with this Act; or

If the court finds:-

- that the subject matter of the dispute is not capable of settlement by arbitration under the laws of Nigeria, or
- that the award is against public policy of Nigeria'.

Q. What Are the Arbitration Institutions in Nigeria?

The following arbitration institutions are operational in Nigeria:

a. The Chartered Institute of Arbitrators UK (Nigerian Branch)
b. The Chartered Institute of Arbitrators Nigeria
c. The Lagos Regional Center for International Commercial Arbitration
d. The International Chamber of Commerce (Nigerian National Committee)
e. The Lagos Court of Arbitration

Anti-Corruption Laws in Nigeria

- Corrupt Practices and other Related Offences Act 2000
- Economic and Financial Crimes Commission (Establishment) Act 2004
- Advanced Fee Fraud and other Fraud Related Offences Act 2006
- Money Laundering (Prohibition) (Amendment) Act 2012
- Failed Bank (Recovery of Debt) and Financial Malpractices in Banks Act 1999
- Bank and other Financial Institution Act 2002
- Fiscal Responsibility Act 2007
- Whistle-blower Protection Act 2015 (waiting to receive the President's Assent)
- Miscellaneous Offences Act
- Code of Conduct Bureau and Tribunal Act
- Dishonoured Cheques (Offences) Act

- Public Procurement Act
- Finance (Control and Management) Act
- Nigeria Extractive Industries Transparency Initiative Act
- Nigerian Financial Intelligence Unit (Establishment) Act
- Penal Code Laws of Federation of Nigeria 2004
- Criminal Code Law of Federation of Nigeria 2004

Anti-Corruption Institutions

- Independent Corrupt Practices Commission
- Economic and Financial Crimes Commission (EFCC)
- Code of Conduct Bureau
- Special Fraud Unit of the Nigerian Police
- Public Complaints Commission

[42] President Muhammadu Buhari was largely elected to office on account of his anti-corruption campaign and antecedents. The Presidency has made a commitment to repatriate as much of the laundered funds as is recovered, into the government treasury, and that all persons found culpable shall be compelled to face legal proceedings. The President has also expressed a desire to merge and consolidate the anti-graft institutions for greater efficiency and accountability. The enabling laws creating the various institutions may, therefore, have to be amended for such consolidation to take effect.

1.6 Forms of Intellectual Property Protection

1.6.1 Trademarks

[43] The Nigerian Trademarks, Patent and Designs Registry under the Commercial Department of the Ministry of Trade and Investments is the authority responsible for trademark applications in Nigeria.

[44] Nigeria is a member of the Paris Convention for the protection of Industrial Property and a treaty member to the Agreement on Trade-Related Aspects of Intellectual Property Rights (TRIPS). The laws currently guiding and regulating trademarks in Nigeria are based on the Trade Marks Act (enacted in 1965), and the Trade Marks Regulations (enacted in 1967). The Trade Marks Act is now referred to as the Nigerian Trade Marks Act (TMA) Cap. T13 (Laws of the Federation of Nigeria (LFN) 2004). Also, applicable in Nigeria is the Merchandise Marks Act Cap. M10 (Laws of the Federation of Nigeria (LFN) 2004).

[45] Nigeria has acceded to the World Intellectual Property Organization (WIPO) treaty that established the African Regional Intellectual Property Office, but there is resistance to importing it into local usage. The supremacy of local Nigerian registration is still preserved.

[46] In recent times, the concept of branding of 'services' has gained ground in Nigeria. Without amending the substantive trademark law that covered 'goods' only, the registration of 'service marks' became effective in Nigeria in April 2007 by the authority of executive fiat from the Federal Minister of Trade and Commerce. Consequently, the international classification of goods and services under the Nice Agreement of 15 June 1957 is now recognized in Nigeria.

1.6.2 Amendments to the Trade Marks Act

[47] In 2018, there was a public reading before the National Assembly of the Federal Republic of Nigeria of Bill No. SB 357. The proposed bill is a Bill for an Act to repeal the Trade Marks Act Cap. T13 LFN 2004 and provide for a comprehensive law on Trade Marks and related matters.

[48] The pending Bill domesticates the Nice Agreement concerning the International Classification of Goods and Services for the purposes of registration of marks. Section 57 of the proposed Bill empowers the Minister of Trade & Investments to give effect to the provisions of the Madrid protocol or of any treaty, convention, arrangement or engagement relating to trademarks to which Nigeria is a party.

[49] The pending Bill to review the TMA makes significant positive changes, such as defensive registration of well-known marks and the recognition of priority applications in Convention countries.

[50] Further, the pending Bill seeks to review the validity period of a trademark to be ten years, and every renewal validity period will also be ten years. Under the pending Bill, each renewal period application should be made not later than six months after the registration of the trademark expires. This is contrary to the current regime under the substantive Act where registration of a trademark is valid for an initial period of seven years and renewable indefinitely for periods of fourteen years.

[51] In addition, under the substantive Act, application for the renewal of registration of a trademark should be made not later than three months before the last registration of the trademark expires.

[52] In the Bill, one of the grounds for revocation of a registered trademark is when the trademark has become the common name in the trade for the product or service for which it is registered.

Patents and Designs

[53] The laws guiding and regulating patents and designs are contained in the Patents and Designs Act, which was enacted in 1971. Nigeria signed the Patent Cooperation Treaty (PCT) in 2003 and deposited the instrument with the WIPO office in 2005. Subsequently, PCT national phase filings are now recognized and undertaken through the local Patents and Trademarks Office (PTO).

[54] WIPO has been assisting the National Office for Technology Acquisition and Promotion to develop a patent desk for the examination of local inventions.

Copyright

[55] Copyright is regulated under the Copyright Act, which was enacted in 1988 and is presently referenced as Cap. 28 Laws of the Federation of Nigeria, 2004. The Nigerian Copyright Commission (NCC) is the body saddled with copyright administrative responsibilities and enforcement of copyright laws. The curbing of piracy is the key focus of the NCC as it continues to constitute a major menace with various obstacles to its prevention. Unfortunately, there is much to be done in the elimination of piracy; copyright, therefore, is not a popular or lucrative area of practice for intellectual property lawyers in Nigeria.

1.7 Recent Developments

[56] The greatest challenge to intellectual property owners as a whole is counterfeiting and product adulteration. The liberalization of regimes controlling the importation of goods due to World Trade Organization treaty obligations has brought these counterfeiting challenges to the fore, especially for developing countries in Africa that rely heavily on imported products. The federal government of Nigeria, therefore, deemed it necessary to tighten the regulatory environment to counteract the menace of product adulteration and counterfeiting.

1.8 Trade Malpractices Act

[57] This Act, which came into effect in 1992, creates certain offences relating to trade malpractices and sets up a Special Trade Malpractices Investigation Panel to investigate such offences. The Act makes it an offence for any person to 'label, package, sell, offer for sale, or advertise any product in a manner that is false or misleading as to its quality, character, brand, name, value, composition, merit, or safety'.

National Agency for Food and Drug Administration and Control Act (NAFDAC Act)

[58] As the successor to the functions of the Department of Food and Drugs Administration, the National Agency for Food and Drug Administration and Control (NAFDAC) was established in 1993 with the functions of, *inter alia*, regulating and controlling the import, export, manufacturing, advertisement, distribution, sale and use of food, drugs, cosmetics, medical devices, bottled water, detergents and chemicals ('regulated products').

[59] Pursuant to the enactment of the NAFDAC Act, no regulated product shall be manufactured, imported, exported, advertised, sold or distributed in Nigeria unless it has been registered in accordance with the provisions of this Act or regulations made under it.

[60] NAFDAC operations have been rather effective in demonstrating a national will to arrest the spate of counterfeiting. Unlike past practice, whereby Intellectual Property ('IP') clients and their lawyers were exposed to protracted discovery processes and litigation to prosecute counterfeiting, the regulator, NAFDAC, has its own enforcement unit that is empowered to seal up any defaulting premises, destroy the offending products and prosecute the case. Among other things, NAFDAC requirements for product registration include evidence of registration in Nigeria of the product trademark (to establish its legitimate proprietor); power of attorney issued by the trademark proprietor to its local agent (who may be a manufacturer or vendor); and a certificate of manufacture and free sale. Among other legislative requirements, an onus is placed on the registered proprietor of trademarks to watch over the marks, as substandard products bearing the trademarks may be assumed to be bona fide products of the trademark owner.

[61] Beyond the scope of NAFDAC, which regulates the products listed above, the Standards Organisation of Nigeria ('SON') plays a role, keeping counterfeit and substandard products under surveillance, but its functions do not extend to the protection of IP rights in the products.

1.9 Enforcement of Rights

1.9.1 Jurisdiction and Venue for Enforcement

[62] The initial forum for dispute settlement available for trademarks is the PTO Registrar Opposition and Administrative Hearing Panel. Thereafter, appeals may proceed to the Federal High Court, and then the Court of Appeal, and ultimately the Supreme Court. The PTO proceedings are particularly important because affidavit evidence provided to the PTO by way of statutory declarations (upon which the PTO bases its ruling) are admissible as evidence in subsequent court litigation on the same subject. At the PTO level, the evidence adduced by statutory declaration is based on factual expositions, without putting the deponent on the witness stand; it is often the case that the deponent does not live in Nigeria. The PTO is better acquainted than the courts with the relevant PTO procedures, so its rulings are more reasoned in accordance with the applicable legal and regulatory regime for intellectual property. Therefore, the evidence adduced and accepted at PTO proceedings also serves as a guide in subsequent court litigation.

[63] The Federal High Court is, however, the primary dispute forum for proprietors of registered trademarks to institute actions for 'infringement' and 'passing off'. Appeals from the Federal High Court can be made to the Court of Appeal and final appeal to the Supreme Court.

[64] Historically, almost all Nigerian trademark disputes were conclusively resolved through PTO proceedings. This created a scarcity of superior court IP case law precedents. However, adequate legal manpower resources are locally available to argue IP cases and British case law precedents are readily admissible because Nigerian IP laws are based on British laws. Case law precedents on European Community trademarks are gradually gaining acceptance, but this is on a case-by-case basis and depends on the circumstances.

1.10 Debtors/Creditors Laws

[65] Nigeria does not have a debt collection system that is deemed effective save for recourse to litigation. There are no special courts.

1.11 Insolvency Law

[66] There are no insolvency laws in Nigeria. The insolvency laws for companies are contained in all the successive company laws of the country, fashioned principally after the British system.

[67] Insolvency laws for banks and bad debtors are principally governed by the Failed Banks (Recovery of Debts) and Financial Malpractices in Banks Act, 1994 and is not patterned after the law of any particular jurisdiction. The Companies and Allied Matters Act provides a framework for corporate asset recovery or realization.

[68] The court of competent jurisdiction on the insolvency of companies and banks is the Federal High Court.

[69] The insolvency of individuals is governed principally by the Bankruptcy Act, 1979.

[70] Voluntary filing for bankruptcy by an individual in order to escape liability to creditors is not recognized.

1.12 Labour Laws

[71] Since 1960, Nigeria has adopted core international labour standards/conventions, which are reflected in the Labour Act. The national labour laws cover free association, right to organize, elimination of forced labour, abolition of child labour and non-discrimination at workplace because of gender.

[72] For companies operating in the rural areas, albeit without any legal obligations on their part, it is considered politically prudent for the unskilled and semi-skilled labour force to be sourced from amongst indigenes within their immediate operational locations. It is also recommended that companies develop Employee Handbooks which comprehensively articulate the Human Resource policies and conditions of employment. With the increased adoption of such Handbook policies, court litigations by employees for unfair dismissal have largely diminished.

[73] There has been recent advocation for the review of the Labour Act to make it more relevant to today's workplace realities. Some of the areas that need to be reviewed include an expansion to its scope of application, extension of maternity leave, inclusion of paternity leave, review of severance pay to include other cash allowances, upward review of fines and penalties for contravention, more stringent protection against child labour, and stricter accountability requirements for employers.

2 REGULATORY FRAMEWORK

2.1 Business Vehicles

[74] Business activities may be undertaken in Nigeria through any of the following vehicles:

- private or public limited liability company;
- unlimited liability company;
- company limited by guarantee;
- foreign company (branch or subsidiary of foreign company);
- partnership/firm;
- sole proprietorship.;
- incorporated trustees; or
- representative office.

[75] Both local and foreign business interests and enterprises must be registered with the Registrar-General of the Corporate Affairs Commission (Registrar of Companies), and comply with the requisite applicable regulations. Therefore, a foreign investor wishing to set up business operations in Nigeria should take all steps necessary to obtain local incorporation of the Nigerian branch or subsidiary as a separate entity in Nigeria for that purpose. Until so incorporated, the foreign business interest may not carry on business in Nigeria or exercise any of the powers of a registered company. The Nigeria-registered company is regarded as separate and distinct from the foreign company.

[76] Pursuant to a Government audit of 'failed' and 'inadequately performed' contracts, a procurement policy (not law) has been adopted to ensure that any foreign company aspiring to undertake and/or execute the contract(s) with the Federal or any State Government must be readily traceable and have a local registration in Nigeria.

[77] The locally incorporated branch or subsidiary company must then apply to the Nigerian Investment Promotion Commission (NIPC) for a Business Permit.

2.2 Exemptions to the General Rule

[78] Where exemption from local incorporation is desired, a foreign company may apply, in accordance with section 80 of the Companies and Allied Matters Act 2020, for exemption from incorporating a local subsidiary if such foreign company belongs to one of the following categories:

- foreign companies invited to Nigeria by or with the approval of the Federal Government of Nigeria to execute any specified individual project;
- foreign companies that are in Nigeria for the execution of specific individual loan projects on behalf of a donor country or international organization;
- foreign government-owned companies engaged solely in export promotion activities; and
- engineering consultants and technical experts engaged in any individual specialist project under contract with any of the governments in the Federation or any of their agencies or with any other body or person, where such contract has been approved by the Federal Government.

[79] The application for exemptions disclosing certain details about the applicant is to be made to the Minister for Trade. If successful, the request of the applicant is granted on such terms and conditions as the Minister for trade may think fit.

[80] An exempted foreign company shall have the status of an unregistered company, and every exemption shall specify the period and, as the case may be, the project for which it is granted, and shall lapse at the end of such period or on the completion of such project.

2.3 Representative Offices

[81] Foreign companies may set up representative offices in Nigeria. A representative office, however, cannot engage in business or conclude contracts or open or negotiate any letters of credit. It can only serve as a promotional and liaison office, and its local operational expenses must be inflowed from the foreign company. A representative office must be registered with the Corporate Affairs Commission (Registrar of Companies).

2.4 Business Formation Procedure

[82] The Companies and Allied Matters Act, 2020 (the Companies Act) is the principal law regulating the registration of business organizations. The administration of the Companies Act is entrusted to the Corporate Affairs Commission (CAC). Briefly, the functions of the CAC include:

- the regulation and supervision of the formation, incorporation, registration, management, and winding up of companies;

- the establishment and upkeep of a suitable and well-equipped Companies Registry;
- the conduct of the investigation into the affairs of any company where the interests of shareholders and the public so demand; and
- the performance of any other functions or activities that may be necessary or expedient in furtherance of the above-stated objectives.

2.5 Reservation of Name

[83] The Companies Act allows the promoters of a new business enterprise or company to file a request for 'Availability of Name' and, if a proposed name is certified available for use, such a name may be reserved for a period of 60 days.

2.6 Minimum Issued Share Capital Requirements and Disclosures in Memorandum of Association

[84] To be registrable, the amount of Minimum Issued Share Capital may not be less than NGN 100,000.00 in the case of private companies or NGN 2,000,000.00 in the case of public companies. A minimum Issued Share Capital of NGN 10 million is required for companies with foreign ownership participation.

[85] The Memorandum of Association must state, *inter alia*, that the subscribers 'shall take among them a total number of shares of a value not less than 25% of the authorized capital and that each subscriber shall write opposite his name the number of shares he takes'.

[86] In recognition of modern-day business realities, the law permits and acknowledges the roles of attorneys, among others, in facilitating business transactions, provided, of course, that this 'agency' arrangement is disclosed. Thus, where subscription is being made to a Company's Memorandum of Association in a representative capacity, section 27(3) of the Companies and Allied Matters Act 2020 mandates that such subscriber must disclose on the face of the document that he is acting in such capacity and 'as attorney for XYZ Limited (name of the principal)'. A number of foreign investors find this approach expedient and have granted Powers of Attorney to local professionals who in turn are able to assist with the processing of the incorporation and other relevant governmental approvals for the establishment of businesses in Nigeria.

2.7 Membership of the Company – Prohibition of Trusts

[87] The Companies Act, like previous legislation, provides that no 'notice of any trust, express, implied or constructive shall be entered on the register of members or be receivable by the CAC'.

2.8 Shares – All Categories of Company Shares to Carry One Vote

[88] Shares with 'weighted' voting rights are prohibited. All shares (i.e., whether ordinary or preferential) issued by a company must carry one vote in respect of each share, and no company may by its articles (i.e., charter/constitution) or otherwise authorize the issue of shares which carry more than one vote in respect of each share or which do not carry any right to vote.

[89] Consequently, preference shareholders are entitled to receive notices and attend all general meetings of the company and may speak and vote on any resolution before the meeting. This is contra-distinctive to most countries where preference shareholders, as quasi creditors, are exempted from voting at general meetings and limited to class meetings.

2.9 Disclosures to be Published in Company Correspondence and Business Premises

[90] Every company is obliged to disclose, on its letterhead papers used in correspondence, the following particulars:

- Name of the company/enterprise.
- Address.
- Registration/Incorporation Number.
- Names of directors and alternate directors (if any).
- Nationality of a foreign director.

[91] This disclosure requirement is a spirited effort to ensure the authenticity of the correspondence by genuine companies and as much as possible to check the activities of fake and non-existing companies.

[92] In addition, the law requires companies/enterprises to ensure that a copy of the Certificate of Registration be displayed in conspicuous positions at their principal and branch offices.

2.9.1 Powers of Attorney

[93] Powers of Attorney are generally expected to be issued on the Company's letterhead and also authenticated by affixing the company seal or stamp. Notary public attestation is also desirable.

2.9.2 Board of Directors

[94] Save for statutorily disqualified persons (minors, lunatics, undischarged bankrupts) the promoters of business ventures in Nigeria are free to appoint directors of their choice, either foreign or Nigerian, and the directors may be resident or non-resident. Directors may be appointed as executive or non-executive directors. Corporate Governance Code for public companies makes it obligatory that non-executive directors should include 'independent' directors, who have no representative stake at all in the company.

[95] Regardless of title adopted, names and particulars of all directors must be filed with the CAC, and their names must reflect on letterheads of the company. All company filings at the CAC must be supported with requisite Board or Shareholder resolutions authorizing the act.

[96] Banks and other financial institutions are not permitted to appoint any director (executive or non-executive) without the prior approval of such candidate by the Central Bank. Any director so approved is prohibited from holding successive terms, as a director, in excess of ten years.

2.9.3 Transactions by Company in Respect of Its Own Shares

Prohibition of financial assistance by a company for acquisition of its Shares

[97] Where a person is acquiring or is proposing to acquire shares in a company, it shall not be lawful for the company or any of its subsidiaries to give financial assistance directly or indirectly for the purpose of that acquisition before or at the same time as the acquisition takes place. The exceptions to the general rule are:

- the lending of money by the company in the ordinary course of business, where the lending of money is part of the ordinary business of a company;
- the provision by a company, in accordance with any scheme for the time being in force, of money for the purchase of, or subscription for, fully-paid shares in the company or its holding company, being a purchase or subscription by trustees of or for shares to be held by or for the benefit of employees of the company, including any director holding salaried employment or office in the company;
- the making by a company of loans to persons, other than directors *bona fide* in the employment of the company with a view to enabling those persons to purchase or subscribe for fully-paid shares in the company or its holding company, to be held themselves by way of beneficial ownership;

- under a scheme of arrangement & compromise, mergers and other corporate restructuring options provided they are sanctioned by the court; and
- where the sole purpose of the assistance is in the best interest of the company, and it was done in good faith.

Acquisition by a company of its own shares

[98] A company is allowed to purchase its own shares, shares including redeemable shares if so, permitted by its articles and approved by the shareholders by special resolution. Furthermore, if a company succeeds in acquiring its shares, payment for the share buyback can only be made from the distributable profits of the company.

Re-issue of shares acquired

[99] Where shares in a company are redeemed, purchased, acquired or forfeited, such shares shall, unless the company by alteration of its articles of association (i.e., governing charter or Constitution) cancels the shares, be available for re-issue by the company.

Acquisition of shares of holding company

[100] A company which is a subsidiary may acquire shares in its holding company where the subsidiary company is concerned as a personal representative or trustee unless the holding company or any subsidiary of it is beneficially interested otherwise than by way of security for the purposes of a transaction entered into by it in the ordinary course of a business which includes the lending of money.

2.9.4 Mandatory Compliance after Incorporation

[101] There are certain requirements under the Companies' Act which must be fulfilled by companies after incorporation. Under the law, it is mandatory for all **financial and non-financial institutions** to make and deliver to the CAC every year, an annual return in a specified form and format, which includes the audited financial accounts.

[102] All **financial institutions** are required by law to submit a 'Statement of Affairs' to the CAC before the commencement of business transactions and also on the first Monday in February and the first Tuesday in August every year in which business is carried out.

[103] The Companies Act recognizes the following primary types of companies:

- 'Company limited by shares', i.e., a company having the liability of its members limited by the Memorandum of Association to the amount, if any, unpaid on the shares respectively held by them.
- 'Company limited by guarantee' without share capital, i.e., a company having the liability of its members limited by the Memorandum of Association to such amount as the members may respectively thereby undertake to contribute to the assets of the company in the event of its being wound up. Apart

from other formalities of incorporation, the 'consent' of the Attorney General of the Federation is required before a company in this category can be registered.

- 'Unlimited Company', i.e., a company not having any limit on the liability of its members.

[104] Each of these primary types of companies may be further categorized into private or public companies. A private company is one that restricts share transfer, limits membership to 50, and prohibits public invitation for subscription to its shares or debentures. A public company could be either listed or unlisted, and a public listed company is one whose shares are listed on the Stock Exchange(s) in Nigeria.

2.9.5 Business Names Registration for Sole Proprietors, Partnerships, and Firms

[105] A 'business name' is defined as 'the name or style under which any business is carried on whether in partnership or otherwise'. In addition, 'a firm' is defined as an unincorporated body of two or more individuals or one or more corporations, who or which have entered into a partnership with one another with a view to carrying on a business for profit.

2.10 Sole Proprietorship

[106] A sole proprietorship must be registered with the CAC as a business name under the Companies and Allied Matters Act.

2.11 Partnerships and Firms

[107] A 'partnership' or 'firm' as a framework for business activity is essentially the same as that of a registered sole proprietor, except that there is more than one party involved.

2.11.1 Limited Liability Partnerships

[108] Under this arrangement, at least one of the partners must be resident in Nigeria. A designated partner shall be responsible for doing all acts, matters and things as are required to be done by the LLP in respect of compliance of the provisions of CAMA 2020, including the filing of any document, return, statement and the like report pursuant to the provisions of CAMA 2020 and as may be specified in the LLP agreement; and liable to all penalties imposed on the LLP for any contravention of those provisions.

[109] For an LLP to be incorporated, two or more persons shall subscribe their names to an incorporation document; and the incorporation document shall be filed with the Commission, and the Commission shall, upon satisfying that all the relevant rules have been complied with, register the incorporation document and give a certificate that the LLP is incorporated by the name specified therein.

[110] The mutual rights and duties of the partners of an LLP, and the mutual rights and duties of an LLP and its partners, shall be governed by the LLP agreement between the partners and In the absence of agreement as to any matter, the mutual rights and duties of the partners and the mutual rights and duties of the limited liability partnership and the partners shall be determined by the provisions relating to that matter as are set out in the Sixteenth Schedule.

[111] A person may cease to be a partner of an LLP in accordance with an agreement with the other partners or, in the absence of an agreement with the other partners as to the cessation of being a partner, by giving a notice in writing of not less than thirty days to the other partners of his intention to resign as a partner.

[112] Every partner of an LLP is, for the purpose of the business of the LLP, the agent of the LLP, but not of other partners. The LLP is expected to maintain books of Accounts, Other Records, and Audit. Every LLP is also expected to file an annual return with the Commission within sixty days of closure of its financial year failing which the limited liability partnership and every designated partner of such limited liability partnership shall each be liable to a penalty in such amount as the Commission shall specify in its regulations. A partner may transfer his profits and losses interest in the limited liability to any person of his choice either wholly or in part. Affairs of Limited Liability Partnership can be investigated, and there is provision for the winding up and dissolution of Limited Liability Partnership.

2.11.2 Limited Partnership

[113] Under this arrangement, the partners must not exceed **twenty** persons; there must be at least one partner known as the General Partner who is liable for all the debts and obligations of the firm and another known as the Limited Partner who at the time of joining the partnership may contribute or undertake to contribute to the assets of the firm, but shall not be liable for the debts and obligations of the firm which exceeds his contribution to the asset of the firm. It is noteworthy that a Limited Partner need not contribute to the asset of the firm if agreed in writing.

2.11.3 Foreign Limited Liability Partnership

[114] A Foreign Limited Liability Partnership incorporated outside Nigeria but is desirous of carrying on business in Nigeria is required to take all necessary steps to be incorporated as a separate entity in Nigeria for that purpose. Until the incorporation is done, it is not allowed to carry on business in Nigeria, have a place or business, or address for service of documents in Nigeria except for receipt of notices and pre-incorporation documents. However, it could apply for an exemption if eligible for exemption subject to the provision of the act and discretion of CAC.

2.12 Incorporated Trustees

[115] A relatively simple procedure has been established for the incorporation of social, scientific, educational, religious, cultural, and other non-profit-making bodies. Under the present statute, these entities may appoint trustees who could, in turn, apply for a certificate of registration as a corporate body with perpetual succession and with the capacity to hold land and to sue and to be sued in its corporate name.

2.13 De-regulation of Equity Structure in Nigerian Enterprises

[116] Effectively, the Nigerian Enterprises Promotion (Repeal) Act Number 7 of 1995 has abolished any restrictions in respect of foreign shareholding participation in Nigerian registered/domiciled enterprises. The only enterprises that are still exempted from free and unrestrained foreign participation are as follows:

- production of arms and ammunition; and
- production of and dealing in psychotropic substances.

3 COMPANIES AND ALLIED MATTERS ACT, 2020

[117] As part of efforts to bring Nigeria's commercial law at par with the global best practices, the Senate passed the Companies and Allied Matters Act (Repeal and Re-enactment) Bill, 2020 in March 2020, and on 7 August 2020, President Muhammadu Buhari assented to the CAMA Bill which became the present Companies and Allied Matters Act 2020 (CAMA 2020).

[118] CAMA 2020 is aimed at ensuring that regulations for Micro, Small and Medium Enterprises are business-friendly, thereby encouraging regulated commercial activities at the grassroots level; reduction in time and cost for setting up a Company; the promotion of financial stability for business entities in Nigeria; and increasing investor confidence in the Nigerian financial sector as well as all sectors of the Nigerian economy.

[119] Highlighted below are some of the salient provisions in the Act –

E-registration

Although the Commission has since adopted e-registration, there was no federal legislation to that effect. The CAMA 2020 expressly provides that the Corporate Affairs Commission is responsible for establishing and using any means of electronic communication to facilitate an automated reservation of names and filing any information contemplated by CAMA. This is aimed at simplifying the means of registering a business in Nigeria as all the hurdles related to the manual registration of a Company would be eliminated.

One-man Company

An individual may form and incorporate a company by complying with the requirements of the CAMA 2020; however, it is noteworthy that this type of company is restricted to a private company. Consequently, an individual cannot form a public company.

Object Clause

CAMA 2020 states that except the articles of association of a company specifically restrict the objects of the company, the objects are unrestricted. The import is that a company is at liberty to amend, add, remove or alter its objects at any point except its article states otherwise.

Minimum Issued Share Capital

The provision on authorized share capital under the repealed act has now been replaced with minimum issued capital, so the term 'authorized share capital' does not arise under CAMA 2020.

Also, the threshold for minimum issued share capital has been upwardly reviewed from NGN 10,000.00 to NGN 100,000.00 in the case of a private company and NGN 500,000.00 to NGN 2 million, for public company.

Consequently, the minimum issued capital of a private company must not at any time fall below NGN 100,000 and NGN 2,000,000 for a public company, a contravention of this will attract penalties for the defaulting company.

Incorporation Documents

The scope of documents required for registration of a company has been expanded under the CAMA 2020. Now, among other things, it is required that if the liability of a member is to be limited by share, the application for registration should contain Statement of Capital and Initial Shareholdings or statement of guarantee if member's liability is to be limited by Guarantee.

Electronic Signature

Where a document or proceeding is required to be authenticated by a company, the CAMA 2020 provides that electronic signature on such document or proceeding shall suffice.

Electronic meeting

A private company will now have the option to hold its general meetings electronically provided that such meetings are conducted in accordance with the articles of the company. The essence of the new provision is to meet the present demands of virtual interactions.

Netting

CAMA 2020 introduced an accounting concept 'Netting' which is used to evaluate and reduce financial risks and burdens. CAMA 2020 states that the contents of a netting agreement are enforceable per their terms, against an insolvent party, a guarantor or other person that may provide security for a party subject to the conditions contained in the applicable netting agreement.

3.1 Guidelines for Foreign Direct Investments and Expatriate Permits

[120] The Nigerian Investment Promotion Commission Act (NIPC Act) came into existence on 16 January 1995. The thrust of this legislation is evidenced by its name and the institution created by it, that is, the Nigerian Investment Promotion Commission (NIPC). Notable among the provisions relating to foreign investments in the NIPC Act are the following:

- a non-Nigerian may invest and participate in the operation of any enterprise in Nigeria;
- an enterprise in which foreign participation is permitted shall, after its incorporation or registration, be registered with the NIPC;
- a foreign enterprise may buy the shares of any Nigerian enterprise in any convertible foreign currency;
- for the purpose of promoting identified strategic or major investments, the NIPC shall, in consultation with appropriate Government agencies, negotiate specific incentive packages for the promotion of investment, as the NIPC may specify; and
- a foreign investor in an enterprise to which this Act applies shall be guaranteed unconditional transferability of funds through an authorized dealer, in the freely convertible currency of: (a) dividends or profits (net of taxes) attributable to the investment; (b) payments in respect of loan servicing where a foreign loan has been obtained; and (c) the remittance of proceeds (net of all taxes), and other obligations in the event of a sale or liquidation of the enterprise or any interest attributable to the investment.

3.2 Guarantees Against Expropriation

[121] Section 25 of the NIPC Act provides that no enterprise shall be nationalized or expropriated by any Government of the Federation; and no person who owns, whether wholly or in part, the capital of any enterprise shall be compelled by law to surrender his interest in the capital to any other persons.

[122] The Federal Government may acquire an enterprise if the acquisition is in the national interest or for a public purpose under a law that makes provision for:

- payment of fair and adequate compensation; and
- a right of access to the courts for the determination of the investor's interest or right and the amount of compensation to which he is entitled.

[123] Any compensation payable under this section shall be paid without undue delay, and authorization for its repatriation in convertible currency shall, where applicable, be issued.

3.3 Business Permit, Expatriate Quota, and Immigration Formalities for Work Permits

[124] The Federal Ministry of Interior is the government authority responsible for expatriate grants to Business Permit, Expatriate Quota, and Work Permits.

[125] A Business Permit, as the name connotes, is the permanent operational/ business permit for the local operation of businesses with foreign investments either as a branch or subsidiary of a foreign company or otherwise.

[126] An Expatriate Quota is the official permit to a company, conveying permission for the company to employ individual expatriates to specifically approved job designations, and also specifying the permissible duration of such employment. The Expatriate Quota forms the basis of work permits for expatriate individuals employed (whose qualifications must fulfil the criteria established for the particular quota position). Expatriate Quota positions are usually granted for two to three years, subject to renewal, except in cases where companies qualify for and are granted not more than one PUR Quota (i.e., Permanent Until Reviewed) position.

[127] As soon as Expatriate Quota positions are granted and the respective individuals to fill the quota positions are recruited, the company must embark on steps to assist the employees in obtaining requisite STR visas that would, on their arrival in Nigeria, be regularized into Work Permit and residency status for the expatriate employees and their accompanying spouses (if any).

3.4 Subject to Regularization Visa

[128] The 'Subject to Regularization' visa (STR) is required by foreigners seeking to take up employment in Nigeria. Section 8(1) of the Immigration Act provides that 'No person, not being a citizen of Nigeria may take up employment in Nigeria other than employment with the Federal or State Government without the consent of the Comptroller-General of Immigration.' Section 33 of the Act further provides that an application must be made to the Comptroller-General by the prospective employer, in writing, confirming that he/she has a vacancy on the expatriate quota and at the same time stating the position in which the prospective employee is to be employed and confirming acceptance of Immigration responsibility.

[129] The employer company applies to the Nigerian embassy or Consular Office in the country where such intending employee/applicant resides, requesting that he (and his accompanying spouse/fiancée/children, if applicable) be granted an STR Visa. In such an application, the employer company undertakes to assume immigration and other responsibilities for the employee (and his accompanying spouse/fiancée/children, if applicable) in Nigeria.

[130] The STR visa is issued at Nigerian missions abroad without reference to the Comptroller- General of Immigration provided that the applicant presents the following to the visa officer:

- national passport or any other acceptable travel document, which must be valid for at least six months on presentation;
- personal Application (IMM 22) in triplicate;
- original letter of employment reflecting his job title (which must correspond with the expatriate quota position as granted to the employer company) and the conditions of such employment duly issued by the prospective employer and three photocopies;
- three copies of the letter of acceptance of offer by the prospective employee;
- originals and three certified true copies of all relevant certificates, diplomas, and other credentials;
- certified translations of the certificates and diplomas (if originals are in a foreign language);
- letter of application from prospective employers confirming acceptance of immigration responsibility (IR);
- photocopy of expatriate quota approval granted to the company with the job title of the employee reflected as one of the expatriate quota positions granted;
- certified copies of marriage or relationship documents in respect of accompanying spouse/fiancé/children; and
- some additional documents, which vary depending on the nationality of the employee, may be requested, e.g., Testimonial of Good Conduct from the municipal authority of the employee's place of residence.

[131] When all these are presented to the visa officer, he will endorse the photocopies and return the originals to the applicant and, if the visa is issued after due Security Clearance, two copies of the completed IMM 22 and of each of all certificates and other credentials presented will be endorsed and sealed in an envelope and addressed to the Comptroller-General of Immigration and then given to the prospective employee together with his passport endorsed with the STR visa. This envelope will be delivered without being tampered with to the Immigration Officer at the office in Nigeria where regularization of the prospective employee would be sought.

[132] The STR visa is normally given for ninety days without reference, during which an application must be made to the Comptroller-General of Immigration, to regularize the stay of the prospective employee, and the person may assume his employment only when such application is approved and a residence work permit granted.

3.5 Registration of Aliens

[133] Having undergone the various legal formalities for residency status, all foreigners are expected to register their presence at the immigration offices closest to their places of residence or occupation.

[134] It should be noted that for this purpose, all the State Immigration Offices are representatives of the Comptroller-General of Immigration and applications for regularization should be made to them, which they would refer accordingly for approval to issue a Combined Expatriate Registration and Aliens Card (CERPAC).

3.6 Temporary Work Permit

[135] Companies and organizations wishing to engage the services of expatriates for short-period assignments are required to apply directly to the Comptroller-General at Abuja, Nigeria for Visa/Entry Permits for such expatriates. This is the Temporary Work Permit Visa (TWP), and it is not issued without reference to the Comptroller-General of Immigration. If such applications are submitted at the Nigerian Missions abroad, they must be referred to the Comptroller-General of Immigration for approval.

[136] The temporary assignments that are eligible for such approval include:

- erection/installation work;
- feasibility studies;
- repairs of machinery/equipment; and
- research work, and such other assignments as may fall in this category.

[137] The TWP visa is given for a period not exceeding three months and may be extended for a further period on application to the Comptroller-General of Immigration who will determine the desirability of such an extension.

[138] It should be noted that the TWP visa is given outside the expatriate quota allocation of the company or organization.

3.7 Multiple Journey Visa

[139] This type of visa is normally issued without reference to the Comptroller-General of Immigration by the Nigerian Missions abroad for a period not exceeding twelve months and maybe for a specified number of journeys within the period granted. It is normally given mostly to non-resident Directors of Nigerian-based companies and other foreign businessmen and women for the purpose of attending meetings frequently and for other frequent visits to pursue business arrangements, or make consultations regarding investment projects.

[140] Multiple journey visas are also given in Nigeria to employees of companies/organizations whose stay has been duly regularized, to enable them to return to their employment whenever they travel either for business or holidays to visit families and friends back home or for pleasure trips to other countries.

[141] Applications for this must be made personally by the employee in Nigeria and not from outside the country. The application must be supported by the employer confirming that the employee is returning to his job, and re-affirming acceptance of immigration responsibility on behalf of the applicant, as well as

showing proof of the continued availability of the expatriate quota position to be occupied.

Quick Checklist Guide for Local Company Registration by Foreign Investors

S/N	*Action*	*Party Responsible*
1.	Advise Solicitor of Name proposed for Company.	Promoters
2.	Conduct a search as to the availability of the proposed Company name, and if available, reserve the name with the Corporate Affairs Commission – pending commencement of registration.	Solicitors
3.	i. Establish partners/shareholders in Company and their respective percentage shareholding participation. ii. Establish initial share capital of Company (minimum of NGN 10 Million). iii. Advise Solicitor of the main business objects and areas of activities of Company.	Promoters
4.	Upon receipt of information required in (3) above, prepare/review drafts of the following documents: i. Shareholders' Agreement. ii. Memorandum and Articles of Association of Company.	
5.	i. Board/Shareholders Resolutions (on Company letterheads) from the foreign (parent) promoter companies authorizing investment in proposed Nigerian Company. ii. Board/Shareholder Resolutions (on Company letterheads) from the foreign (parent) promoter companies nominating the designated Directors to the Board of the Nigerian Company. iii. Full names, addresses and nationalities of the proposed Directors and copies of the data pages of their international passports. iv. Consent Letters of nominated director(s). v. Copies of Certificate of Registration of each Non-Nigerian Promoter Company in its country of domicile.	Promoters Promoters Promoters Promoters Promoters Promoters Promoters

S/N	*Action*	*Party Responsible*
	vi. Where the company's objects and services require technical and specialized skills, supporting documents for registration must include recognized Certificate(s) of Proficiency in the particular field of service, in respect of at least one of the subscribers/promoters. If the certificate is in a language other than English, then it must be accompanied by its English translation (*Consular Legalization is NOT required). vii. Foreign Shareholder(s) to grant Powers of Attorney to its Solicitors in Nigeria, enabling them to act as its Agent in executing incorporation and other statutory documents, pending the grant of Business permit.	
6.	i. Company Incorporation and obtaining Certificate of Incorporation from the Corporate Affairs Commission. ii. NIPC Business Permit Certificate – (required for companies with foreign shareholding). iii. VAT and FIRS tax registration – (Tax Identification No is required for Bank Account opening). iv. Business Permit from Federal Ministry of Interior.	Solicitors
7.	Official inflow of non-resident equity funds to Nigeria from foreign shareholder (as Transferor) to Nigerian Company (as Transferee/Beneficiary) for Purpose (equity investment) and obtain Certificate of Capital Importation (CCI).	Foreign Shareholder and Receiving bank in Nigeria

3.8 Exchange Control and Currency Regulation

[142] Documentation formalities for capital importation by foreign investors have been simplified. Prior approvals of the Federal Ministry of Finance for conferment of 'Approved Status' on such investments are no longer required, and capital importation is now remitted directly into the local currency account of the Nigerian subsidiary/affiliate at the prevailing Inter-Bank Foreign Exchange Market (IFEM) rate.

3.9 Equity Contributions in Cash

[143] Equity investments in cash by a foreign investor can be consummated by such investor transferring his equity allocation into Nigeria, through any of the duly licensed banks operating in the country. The remittance instructions should clearly stipulate the following:

- name of transferor (i.e., foreign investor);
- amount transferred;
- purpose (i.e., equity/capital investment);
- beneficiary (i.e., the appropriate Nigerian affiliated/subsidiary enterprise); and
- board resolution of the local beneficiary company authorizing the investment.

[144] The money is credited to the recipient Nigerian enterprise, at the local currency equivalent, in accordance with rates derived from the Inter-Bank Foreign Exchange Market (IFEM).

[145] Immediately thereafter, the receiving Nigerian bank would issue the investor with a 'Certificate of Capital Importation' ('CCI') for the amount received, and the money can immediately start to be utilized by the Nigerian affiliate/subsidiary for operational and capital requirements.

[146] The 'Certificate of Capital Importation' confers a right to repatriate dividend yields and the proceeds obtained on a sale/disposal of the investment in question, subject, of course, to compliance with the tax and other applicable regulation on the subject.

3.10 Equity Contributions Other than Cash

[147] Where capital is imported in the form of equipment/machinery or raw materials, the 'Certificate of Capital Importation' shall be issued subject to the following documentation requirements:

- original Clean Report of Findings;
- original Bill of Lading;
- original Bill of Entry;
- original Import Duty Report (IDR); and
- board resolution of the local beneficiary company authorizing the investment.

3.11 Guidelines on External Loans to Nigerian Subsidiaries/Branches of Foreign Business Operations

3.11.1 Loan Importation

[148] Within the various laws and regulations currently applicable, an external loan transaction could be consummated with the following steps:

- offer letter of loan from the lender to the borrower (denominated in foreign currency);
- board resolution(s) authorizing the foreign-currency-denominated loan, i.e., in the customary corporate manner for local borrowings;
- execution of a formal loan agreement setting out the terms of borrowings (i.e., principal amount, tenure, applicable interest rate, and so on); however, in this regard, it would be pertinent that the debt instrument and obligations be denominated in convertible foreign currency; and
- remittance instructions accompanying the funds' inflow, through an authorized dealer (i.e., a duly licensed local bank), should clearly reflect the purpose of transfer as loan.

[149] The remittance instructions accompanying the funds should also indicate the following:

- name of transferor (i.e., the lender);
- amount transferred (USD or other freely convertible international foreign currency);
- name and address of beneficiary (local borrower); and
- purpose (loan importation).

[150] This information would enable the receiving bank to issue the ensuing 'Certificate of Capital Importation' and thereafter notify the Foreign Exchange and Trade Relations Department of the Central Bank and the Nigerian Investment Promotion Commission for record and monitoring purposes.

3.11.2 Loan Repayment

[151] External loan repayment requires the following documents:

- evidence of loan importation into Nigeria, *vide* 'certificate of loan importation'; the certificate should be duly authenticated by the bank that issued it, if not issued by the remitting bank;
- certified true copy of loan agreement showing the schedule of repayment;
- schedule of the drawdown of the loan;
- demand note (invoice) for repayment;
- completed and approved Form 'A', i.e., an official form designed for banking transactions; and
- evidence of tax payment on interest income.

3.12 Miscellaneous Exchange Control Issues

3.12.1 Prohibition of Importation and Exportation of the Local Nigerian Currency

[152] The importation and exportation of the Naira are prohibited. However, Nigerian residents are allowed to hold a maximum amount of NGN 5,000.00 for settlement of local expenses immediately on their return to Nigeria from an overseas trip.

3.12.2 Declaration of Certain Foreign Currency Imports

[153] Foreign currency imports of USD 10,000 and above or its equivalent are required to be declared on Form TM for statistical purposes only.

3.12.3 Expatriate Home Remittance

[154] Foreign nationals are allowed to remit 100% of their salaries net of tax as Personal Home Remittance (PHR). However, evidence of income earned and taxes paid must be provided to the banks before remittances are made.

3.12.4 Royalties, Technical Services, and Management Fees

[155] The remittable limits of fees for the licence of Technical Know-How Agreements range between 1% and 5% of net sales value. Similarly, permissible management service fees range between 1% to 5% of a company's profit before tax. The certificate of registration issued by the National Office of Technology Acquisition and Promotion (NOTAP) is one of the documents required for the purpose of procuring foreign exchange for this type of transaction. The initial duration of such agreements shall be three years except for the hotel industry and agro-allied enterprises, where the duration of ten years and five years, respectively, shall be allowed.

[156] Remittable consultancy fees is allowed up to a maximum of 5% of the project cost in cases of projects of very high technology content for which indigenous expertise is not available. Service agreements for such high technology ventures must include a schedule for the training of Nigerian personnel for an eventual takeover. In addition, Nigerian professionals must be involved in the project implementation from inception.

3.12.5 Foreign Guarantees/Currency Deposits as Collateral for Naira Loans

[157] The erstwhile prohibition of foreign guarantees for Naira denominated loans as contained in the Central Bank of Nigeria Monetary Policy Circular Number 23, Amendment Number 3 of April 1989, has been annulled by Central Bank Monetary Policy Circular Number 36 for fiscal years 2002/2003. However, any request for such guarantees shall be subject to prior approval by the Central Bank of Nigeria.

3.12.6 Anti-Money Laundering Rules for Currency Transactions

[158] A person who imports foreign currency in excess of USD 10,000 by cash and deposits such money into the domiciliary account with an authorized dealer shall only be entitled to make cash withdrawals from that account.

[159] No person in Nigeria shall make or accept cash payment whether denominated in foreign currency or not for the purchase and acquisition of landed properties, stocks, shares, debentures, all forms of negotiable instruments, and motor vehicles. Payments for those items must be made by means of bank transfers or checks drawn on banks in Nigeria.

[160] To ensure full compliance with the law, all banks have been directed to appoint Compliance Officers whose duty shall be to ensure that the provisions of the law are complied with. The compliance officers shall report through the Chief Executive of the bank to the Central Bank of Nigeria (CBN) all breaches of the law in such manner as the CBN may from time to time prescribe.

3.12.7 Bank Verification Number

[161] The Central Bank directed account holders in all Nigerian banks to register before October 2015, for a Bank Verification Number ('BVN') that uniquely identifies all multiple accounts held in that person's name. The biometric features are intended to facilitate trails of money to identifiable persons.

3.13 Incentives for Foreign Investment

[162] The government has progressively introduced a number of incentives designed to promote investment, employment, product mix, and various other aspects of the industry. These incentives fall within the following broad categories:

- fiscal measures on taxation;
- effective protection of local industries with import tariff;
- export promotion of Nigerian-made products; and
- foreign currency facility for international trade.

[163] Enterprises that fulfil the necessary criteria are free to apply for the Pioneer Status (i.e., Tax Holiday Status), which is 100% tax-free period of three years for pioneer industries that produce products declared as 'pioneer products' under the Industrial Development (Income Tax Relief) Act. The Industrial Development (Income Tax Relief) Act, Cap. 17 Laws of Nigeria, 2004, declares a number of industries as pioneer industries. Thus, any company whose products fall within the categorized industries could be conferred with Pioneer Status. For the avoidance of doubt, it must be explained that this designation is not necessarily a reflection that a company was a pioneer per se in the industry, as several companies within the same pioneer industry classification could qualify for Pioneer Status. Where the activities of a company include the production of pioneer and non-pioneer products, the tax relief available on conferment of Pioneer Status would be restricted to income derived from the pioneer products only. Under the current industrial policy, conferment of Pioneer Status presently accords a company relief from income tax liability for a period of up to three years (i.e., tax holiday status).

[164] Finally, it should be noted that even if a company's activities and/or products are classified within pioneer industries, the grant of Pioneer Status is not automatic. The criteria for granting Pioneer Status are related and/or based on the following considerations:

- The amount of underlying capital investment in a company must be verifiable by physical inspection and supported by a report of the Industrial Inspectorate Division of the Federal Ministry of Industries before a Pioneer Certificate is granted.
- The socio-economic advantages of a company's activities to the Nigerian economy as set out in its Feasibility Study are also an important consideration.

[165] The incentives itemized here are in no way exhaustive, and neither are the quantum nor percentage of relief mentioned fixed for all times. The would-be investor is, therefore, advised to ascertain the current operative figures at the time of making his investment.

4 FREE TRADE ZONES IN NIGERIA

[166] The creation of a Free Trade Zone (or Free Zones) in Nigeria was designed to attract foreign direct investment, promote exports, enhance trade and industrialization, and contribute to the economic growth and development of Nigeria. An enterprise operational in a free trade zone is exempted from the standard commercial laws and regulations applicable all over the country of Nigeria, especially laws and regulations pertaining to taxation and customs duties. In return for these exemptions, it is anticipated that the free zone enterprises would boost the Nigerian economy and national exports. Free trade zones are referred to as the export processing zones of Nigeria.

[167] The incorporation and activities of Free Zones are primarily governed by the Nigeria Export Processing Zone Authority (NEPZA or the Authority), which was established by the Nigeria Export Processing Zone Act (NEPZ Act). Another key regulatory body is the Oil and Gas Export Free Zone Authority dedicated to the Oil and Gas Free Trade Zone (OGEFZ).

[168] The Nigeria Industrial Revolution Plan[1] (NIRP) evaluated areas where Nigeria has some level of regional or international comparative advantage. These are

[1] NIRP - Release 1.0 (January 2014).

the areas of Agribusiness & Agro-Allied; Solid Minerals & Metals; Oil & Gas related Industry; and Construction, Light Manufacturing & Services. However, the free zones are also open to other investments based on merit and sustainability.

4.1 Application Laws and Regulations

[169] In addition to the primary legislation governing Free Trade Zones, each Free Trade Zone has its regulations. Below is a list of laws and subsidiary legislation primarily governing the activities of free trade zones in Nigeria:

- Nigeria Export Processing Zones Authority Act
- Oil and Gas Export Free Zone Act
- Free Zones (Monitoring and Regulations) Order 2014
- Free Zones (Tariffs and Other Chargers) Order
- Investment Procedures, Regulations and Operational Guidelines for Free Zones in Nigeria, 2004 (NEPZA Regulations)
- OGEFZ Regulations (2003)
- Oil and Gas Export Free Zone (Special Import Provisions) Order 2003
- Central Bank of Nigeria Guidelines for Banking Operations in the Free Zones in Nigeria, 2016

4.2 Licensing of Free Trade Zones

[170] The Nigeria Export Processing Zones Authority (the Authority) and applicable Zone Management are responsible for the issuance of licenses to free zone operators. The Authority/Zone Management may grant approval for one or more of the following Licences:

- *Free Zone Developers Licence*
  A Free Zone Developers License is granted by the Authority to either a public, private entity or a combination of the two for the establishment, operation and management of a Free Zone in Nigeria under the supervision, monitoring and regulation by the Nigeria Export Processing Zones Authority.
- *Free Zone Enterprise Licence*
  A Free Zone Enterprise License is granted by the Authority/Zone Management for an enterprise to undertake an approved activity within a Free Zone. These activities could be manufacturing, trading or the provision of a service.
- *Export Processing Factory/Export Processing Farm Licence*
  An Export Processing Factory/Export Processing Farm License is granted by the Authority to an export-oriented manufacturing enterprise of a farm located in the customs territory which has the capacity to export over 75% of its production.

[171] In determining eligibility for a Licence, the Authority/Zone Management may consider the following:

- The activities which the applicant proposes to engage shall be in consonance with the free zone approved activities.
- The proposed activities to be carried out shall add value to and be consistent with, the development programme for the Free Zone.
- The applicant shall comply with the provisions of the Act and applicable Rules and Regulations that may be put in place by the Authority/Zone management from time to time.
- The technical, financial and managerial capabilities of the applicant.
- The applicant's experience and track record.
- The level of foreign direct investment proposed by the applicant and guidelines for free zone developers, evidence of title to a suitable land area free of encumbrances for the intended purpose.

4.3 Existing Free Trade Zones

[172] Based on the information provided by NEPZA on its web portal, there are currently twenty-two active free zones in Nigeria, with some offering industry-specific purposes and others for more general purposes. However, there are twenty free zones that are inactive or undergoing construction. There are over 300 zone enterprises licensed to operate in free zones of Nigeria.

[173] The active free zones by location are:

- Adamawa State – Sebore Farms EPZ
- Akwa Ibom State – ALSCON EPZ
- Cross River State – Calabar Free Trade Zone (CFTZ)
- Enugu State – Enpower Free Trade Zone
- Federal Capital Territory, Abuja –
  - Centenary Economic City
  - Abuja Tech. Village Free Zone
  - Newrest Airline Service & Logistic FTZ
- Kano State – Kano Free Trade Zone (KFTZ)
- Lagos State
  - Newrest Airline Services & Logistic EPZ
  - Dangote Industries Free Zone
  - Ladol Free Zone
  - Lagos Free Trade Zone
  - Lekki Free Trade Zone
  - Nigeria Aviation Handling Company (NAHCO)
  - Nigeria International Commerce City (Eko Atlantic)
  - Snake Island Integrated Free Zone
  - Tomaro Industrial Park
  - Quits Aviation Services FZ

- Pan African Catering Services FZ
- NASCO FZ
- Alaro City Lekki Free Zone
- Ogun State – Ogun Guangdong Free Trade Zone

4.4 Local Content Development and Policy in Nigeria

4.4.1 Nigerian Oil and Gas Industry Content Development Act

[174] To consolidate the objective of increasing indigenous participation in the Nigerian Oil and Gas Industry, the Nigerian Government introduced the Nigerian Oil and Gas Industry Content Development Act 2010 (the '***Local Content Act***') which has brought about a significant increase in indigenous participation within the industry.

[175] The Local Content policy prescribes minimum thresholds for Nigerian participation in activities within the industry through the utilization of Nigerian human and material resources and services in the upstream sector of the industry. This includes all activities connected with the exploration, development, exploitation, transportation and sale of Nigerian crude oil and gas resources.

[176] The policy affords Nigerian Independent Operators the opportunity of first consideration in the award of oil blocks, oil field licenses, oil lifting licenses and in all projects for which a contract is to be awarded in the Nigerian oil and gas industry.

[177] Exclusive consideration is also provided to Nigerian indigenous service companies which demonstrate ownership of equipment, Nigerian personnel and capacity to execute such work to bid on land and swamp operating areas of the Nigerian oil and gas industry for contracts and services. In furtherance of ensuring greater stability and growth in the Nigerian Oil and Gas sector, the Act further mandates that a minimum of 10% (of total revenue accruing from operations in Nigeria) is retained. Furthermore, the policy prescribes ownership of controlling shares by Nigerians in Oil and Gas service companies, which effectively prescribes less than 100% foreign ownership. By this, the government has tried to achieve a target of 70% use of indigenous labour, materials and resources in all oil and gas projects across the country.

4.4.2 Proposed Nigerian Content Development and Enforcement Act

[178] In December 2019, the House of Representatives commenced the first reading of the Nigerian Content Development and Enforcement Bill (the 'NCDE Bill'). The NCDE Bill seeks to repeal the Nigerian Oil and Gas Industry Content Development Act 2010 ('the Act') and in addition to the Oil and Gas Industry, broaden the scope of its application to cover other industries/sectors, such as Information and Communication Technology (ICT), Mining, Power Sector and Construction. The Bill seeks to ensure that first consideration should be given to Nigerian operators in the issuance of licences and permits in the designated sectors whiles enterprises or individuals desirous of carrying out business in any area of the Nigerian economy shall give priority in terms of awards of contracts and employment to Nigerian indigenous businesses and individuals.

[179] Highlighted below are the major implications of the NCDE Bill, on each affected Sector as well as general provisions:

Oil and Gas sector

- The NCDE Bill establishes the Nigerian Oil and Gas Content Development and Enforcement Board to approve, evaluate and receive the Nigerian content plan and reports submitted by Operators in the Oil and Gas Industry. In conjunction with the Minister of Oil and Gas, the Board is empowered to make regulations setting out targets for the full utilization of indigenous companies as Operators in the sector.
- The NCDE Bill provides for training of local skills within the sector. Operators within the sector are required to maintain offices in all communities where they have significant operations. Local Operators shall be given first consideration in the award of oil blocks, oil licences and contracts in the oil and gas industry.
- The submission of a Nigerian Content Plan (depicting how the Operators intend to give first consideration to Nigerian goods and services in the course of their operation) in the award of any contracts to an Operator will be mandatory. A Certificate of Authorization will be issued as *prima facie* evidence that the Plan is in conformity with the provisions of the NCDE Bill.
- Operators are to have a five-year succession plan wherein Nigerians are made understudies to expatriates holding certain positions, and are groomed to assume such positions.
- Foreign employees of Operators are mandated to obtain work permits in line with the expatriate quota approved by the Board.
- Operators are mandated to submit a list of all contracts, subcontracts and purchase orders exceeding USD 1,000,000 to the Board.
- Contracts with a total budget exceeding USD 1,000,000 are mandated to have a Labour Clause, stipulating a minimum percentage of Nigerian labour in specific cadres, as may be approved by the Board; however, all operators and companies operating in the Nigerian oil and gas industry shall employ only Nigerians in their junior and intermediate cadre or any other corresponding grades designated by the operator or company.
- International or multinational companies in the oil and gas industry working through their Nigerian subsidiaries are mandated to demonstrate that a minimum of 50% of equipment deployed for execution of work, are owned by the local entity.

Information and Communication Technology (ICT) Sector

- The NCDE Bill establishes the National Office for Nigerian Content on Information and Communications Technology, which shall be responsible for implementing the local content obligations of the ICT sector.
- Exclusive consideration shall be given to Nigerian indigenous companies who demonstrate the requisite capacity, with regards to the grant of licences, leases, permits, and other right-vesting instruments in relation to the ICT sector.
- The application of these provisions shall extend to all Federal Ministries, Departments and Agencies, Federal Government-Owned Companies (fully or partially owned), Federal Institutions/Public Corporation, Private Sector Institutions, Business Enterprises and individuals carrying out activity in any area in ICT. Also, it will apply to all existing or future requirements for periodic accreditation and renewal of licences of ICT Companies, Original Equipment Manufacturers (OEM), Original Design Manufacturers (ODM), NITDA registered entities and NCC licensees; and in the grant of approvals or permits for the establishment of new manufacturing or assembly plants, software houses, ICT parks and allied facilities.

Solid Minerals and Mining Sector

- The NCDE Bill establishes the Department of Nigerian Content Development and Enforcement on Solid Minerals ('the Department') which shall be responsible for the implementation of the local content obligations of the solid minerals and mining sector.
- All permits, licenses and leases arrangements, agreements, contracts or memorandum of understanding relating to any operation or transaction in the Solid Minerals, shall be in conformity with the regulations to be issued by the Department.
- Exclusive consideration shall be given to Nigerian indigenous companies who demonstrate the capacity to execute any work in the Solid Minerals Mining Sector when all instruments conferring rights of operation in the Solid Minerals Mining in Nigeria are to be issued.
- A 5% development charge of the monetary value of the proceeds of a sale by any operator in the sector is to be paid into a Fund to be known as 'National Solid Mineral Development Fund'. The Fund shall be administered by the Department to promote Nigerian Content in the Solid Minerals Sector especially in respect of the execution of projects that will enhance acquisition of equipment and technologies by Nigerians to independently exploit solid mineral resources.
- Operators are to submit to the Board within thirty days from the end of each quarter a list of all contracts, subcontracts and purchase orders exceeding USD 1,000,000 (or such other limit prescribed by the Board) awarded by it in the previous quarter.
- All operators or project promoters in the sector shall submit a Nigerian Content Plan which shall contain an Employment and Training Plan.

- All Operators in the sector are mandated to receive the approval of the Board before applying to the Ministry of Internal Affairs for an expatriate quota.
- Contracts or projects in the sector shall contain a labour clause mandating the use of a minimum percentage of Nigerian labour in specific cadres.

Power Sector

- The NCDE establishes the Nigerian Content Development and Enforcement Agency on Power ('the Agency') which shall be responsible for the implementation of the local content obligations of the power sector.
- Exclusive consideration will be given to Nigerian indigenous companies who demonstrate the capacity to carry out the relevant activity, in the issuance of licences, permits, leases and other instruments vesting right of operation in the Power Sector of Nigeria.
- In an instance where local capacity and or materials for any power sector contract are inadequate, the Board may grant an approval for a waiver for the work to be undertaken by a foreign entity; provided that such approval shall not be valid for more than three years.
- Contracts with a total budget exceeding a threshold to be set by the Agency shall have a Labour Clause mandating the use of a minimum percentage of Nigerian labour in specific cadres.
- A 2% charge of the monetary value of the unit purchased will be borne by a final consumer. This charge will be paid into a Fund to be known as 'National Power Development Fund' which shall be administered by the Agency together with the Nigerian Electricity Regulatory Commission to promote Nigerian Content in the Power Sector.

Construction Sector

- Exclusive consideration will be given to Nigerian indigenous companies who demonstrate the capacity to execute the relevant work in the Construction Industry, and all Federal Government-owned entities will be mandated to comply with this requirement.

General Provisions

- Operators, project promoters, alliance partners and Nigerian Indigenous Operators are mandated to patronize insurance and legal services in Nigeria for the execution of their operations.
- Operators engaged in business in any of the selected sectors are to retain the services of the Nigerian Financial institutions or organizations except the transaction relates to securing loans at a lower rate compared to what is obtainable in the financial sector in Nigeria.
- It would be unlawful for a governmental agency to issue visas to a foreigner seeking to work in Nigeria, where the skill being imported is readily available in Nigeria.

Nigerian Oil and Gas Industry Content Development Amendment Bill

[180] It is noteworthy that the Nigerian Senate is deliberating on another local content-focused bill, the Nigerian Oil and Gas Industry Content Development Amendment Bill (the Senate NOGIC Amendment Bill), which proposes to amend and clarify, rather than repeal, the Local Content Act. The Senate NOGIC Amendment Bill has passed its second reading.

[181] Highlighted below **is** a summary of the amendments to be introduced by the Senate NOGIC Bill:

- A Nigerian Company is defined as a Nigerian resident incorporated company with its entire shareholders, directors and asset owners made up solely of persons who are of Nigerian descent. This is in contrast with the description in the Act which describes a Nigerian Company as a company incorporated in Nigeria with not less than 51% equity shares held by persons who are of Nigerian descent.
- The first consideration is to be given to Nigerian indigenous operators in the award of Oil Block Licences, Oil Field Licences, Oil Lifting Licences and in all other contract awarding aspects of the Nigerian Oil and Gas Industry.
- Nigerian owned indigenous service companies that have shown ownership of equipment, qualified personnel and the capacity to execute work on land and swamp operating areas of the Nigerian oil and gas industry, would be given exclusive consideration.
- Nigerian indigenes shall be exclusively considered for the employment of junior and intermediate cadre employees.
- Indigenous insurance, reinsurance and legal firms would be given exclusive engagement consideration, for advisory and insurances services to oil and gas operators.
- The minimum indigenous content requirements contained in the Nigerian Indigenous Content Plan shall be applicable to all participants in the oil and gas industry.
- All Indigenous Content Plans must be pre-qualified and pre-approved by the Nigerian Content Development and Monitoring Board ('the Board') using the first consideration, exclusivity and other indigenous content development criteria before any commercial award can occur in the Nigerian Oil and Gas Industry.

[182] A sum equal to 1% of every contract awarded in the upstream of the Oil and Gas Industry must be deducted at source and paid into the Nigerian Content Development Fund. The Board shall spend an amount not exceeding 10% of the contributions in the Fund, on its general and administrative operations. Also, 70% of the Fund is to be disbursed to qualified Nigerian Indigenous companies to undertake in-country capacity development in the oil and gas industry.

5 GENERAL TAXATION REGIME

5.1 List of Approved Taxes and Levies for the Three Tiers of Government

[183] The 1997 Budget speech directed the Joint Tax Board (JTB) to publish a list of all taxes and levies that can be legitimately collected by each tier of government in Nigeria. The directive was a result of several complaints by the business community arising from a multiplicity of taxes and the employment of services of tax consultants in pursuit of the States' Accelerated Revenue Generation Schemes.

[184] A list of taxes and levies approved for collection by the three tiers of government has now been incorporated into the Taxes and Levies (Approved List for Collection) Act. The list of the approved taxes and levies are as follows.

5.2 Federal Taxes

[185] The following taxes are collectable by the Federal Government:

- companies income tax;
- withholding tax on companies, residents of the Federal Capital Territory, Abuja (FCT Abuja) and non-resident individuals;
- petroleum profits tax;
- value added tax;
- education tax;
- capital gains tax on corporate entities, residents of the FCT Abuja and non-resident individuals;
- stamp duties on corporate entities and residents of the Abuja FCT;
- National Information Technology Development Fund (NITDF) Levy;
- personal income tax in respect of: (a) armed forces personnel; (b) police personnel; (c) FCT Abuja; (d) external affairs; and (e) non-resident individuals; and
- stamp duties (instruments executed by companies and residents of the FCT Abuja).

5.3 States Taxes and Levies

[186] The following taxes/levies are collectable by state governments:

- personal income tax: (a) pay-as-you-earn (PAYE); (b) direct (self and government) assessment;
- withholding tax (individuals only);
- capital gains tax (individuals only);

- stamp duties (on instruments executed by individuals);
- pools betting, lotteries, gaming, and casino taxes;
- road taxes;
- business premises registration and renewal levy: (a) urban areas (as defined by each state); and (b) rural areas;
- development levy (individuals only) on all taxable individuals;
- naming of street registration fee in state capitals;
- right of occupancy fees on lands in urban areas of each state; and
- rates in markets where state finances are involved.

5.4 Local Taxes and Levies

[187] Taxes/levies collectable by local governments include:

- shops and kiosks rates;
- tenement rates;
- on and off liquor licenses;
- slaughter slab fees;
- marriage, birth, and death registration fees;
- naming of streets registration fees (excluding state capitals);
- right of occupancy fees on lands in rural areas, excluding that collectable by the Federal and State Governments;
- market levies (excluding markets where state finances are involved);
- motor park levies;
- domestic animal licenses;
- bicycle, truck, canoe, wheelbarrow, and cart fees other than mechanically propelled trucks;
- cattle tax;
- merriment and road closure levies;
- radio/television (other than radio/TV transmitter) licenses and vehicle radio licenses (to be imposed by the local government of the state in which the car is registered);
- wrong parking charges;
- public convenience, sewage, and refuse disposal fees;
- customary burial ground permit fees;
- religious places establishment permit fees; and
- signboard/advertisement permit fees.

5.5 Transaction Taxes

[188] The Finance Act 2019, which became effective on 1 February 2020, was introduced to reform Nigeria's tax laws to align with global best practices, support medium- and small-scale enterprises in line with the Nigerian Ease of Doing Business Reforms, incentivize investments in infrastructure and capital markets, and raise government revenues. This Act made amendments to the existing tax laws in Nigeria, which will be reflected in subsequent paragraphs.

5.5.1 Withholding Tax

[189] For both the individual and company tax, there is a system of withholding tax in lieu of the taxpayers making the final tax returns, to help the taxpayers to fulfil their tax obligation in a gradual process. It also helps to build an information bank by the tax office to combat tax evasion. The widening of the tax base has been the harvest of the system since it was introduced in Nigeria. The prevailing rates of withholding tax for individuals and companies are as specified below.

5.5.2 Applicable Rates

[190] The following rates are applicable:

Types of Payment	*Individuals (%)*	*Companies (%)*
Dividend, Interest, and Rent	10	10
Royalties	5	10
Commission, Consultancy, Technical, service fees	5	10
Management Fees	5	10
Construction (Roads, Building, Road and Bridges)	5	2.5
Contracts other than sales in the ordinary course of business	5	5
Directors' Fees	10	N/A
Hire of equipment	10	10

5.6 Capital Gains Tax

[191] As of 1996, gains accruing to a taxpayer on the disposal of a 'chargeable asset' are subject to a capital gains tax at 10%. Chargeable assets are defined to include all forms of property, whether situated in Nigeria or not, including:

- options, debts, and incorporeal property generally;
- any currency other than Nigerian currency; and
- any form of property created by the person disposing of it, or otherwise coming to be owned without being acquired.

[192] It should be noted that shares and stocks of every description have been exempted from capital gains taxation as chargeable assets with effect from January 1998. The underlying rationale was to boost the capital market by encouraging dealings in stocks and shares.

[193] By virtue of the provisions of the Finance Act, Capital Gains Tax would no longer be applicable to assets sold or transferred to a related party in a restructuring exercise or related party transaction, when such acquired assets are disposed of within 365 days from the date of restructuring.

5.7 Value Added Tax

[194] Government has approved the introduction with effect from January 1994 of value added tax (VAT) to replace the existing sales tax. By virtue of the provisions of the Finance Act, a VAT rate of 7.5% shall be applied to specified categories of taxable goods and services. VAT-able goods have been defined by the Finance Act to include incorporeal property, which had been a controversial subject in prior years.

[195] The Finance Act further provides that companies with an annual turnover of NGN 25 Million or less are exempted from registering for and charging VAT, rendering a monthly return of its sales and purchases, and from the penalties associated with non-compliance. Also, services rendered by microfinance banks are VAT exempt.

[196] In allocating VAT on services provided by a non-resident company to a Nigerian company, the Finance Act provides the application of a 'place of supply rule' to the effect that VAT shall be paid on every service supplied (either locally or imported) to a Nigerian-based customer and enjoyed in Nigeria.

5.8 Education Tax

[197] Since 1995, an education tax of 2% of assessable profits is imposed on all companies incorporated in Nigeria. The tax is a social obligation by all companies to improve the standard of education facilities in the country.

5.9 Stamp Duties

[198] The administration of stamp duties is jointly carried out by the State and Federal tax authorities, depending on the type and nature of document.

[199] Stamp duties are regarded as transaction taxes, and the rates chargeable would depend on the classification of the document. Some documents attract stamp duties on a flat rate basis while others are assessed ad valorem.

5.10 Petroleum Profits Tax

[200] The Finance Act introduced a 10% Withholding Tax rate payable on dividends paid out of petroleum profits.

5.11 Personal Income Tax

5.11.1 Basis of Liability to Personal Income Tax

[201] A taxpayer is liable to tax in Nigeria on the aggregate amounts of his incomes from sources inside or outside Nigeria; that is, on his global income.

5.11.2 Residency Test

[202] From 1990, the 183-day test utilized to establish the taxability of employment income is to be calculated on a twelve-month period commencing in a calendar year and ending either within the same calendar year concerned or the following calendar year.

5.11.3 Income from Employment

[203] As regards the taxation of income from employment, the law is concerned with the totality of the remuneration, earnings, or benefits in cash or kind obtained by an employee. The particular nomenclature or description of what an employee gets is irrelevant. What is crucial is whether such earnings or benefit becomes due to an employee as a result of his employment. Consequently, any salary, wages, fees, allowances, or other gains or profits from employment, including gratuities, compensation, bonuses, premiums, benefits, or other perquisites allowed, given, or granted by an employer to an employee are taxable. However, to this general rule are a number of exceptions.

[204] In computing the income or loss of an individual, certain outgoings and expenses are specifically allowed.

Tax Identification Number

[205] All taxable persons (body corporate, trustee, partnership, etc.) are mandated to provide a Tax Identification Number as a precondition for opening a bank account and for continued operations of its bank account in respect of its business operations.

5.12 Companies Income Tax

5.12.1 Basis of Liability to Companies Income Tax

[206] In Nigeria, tax is payable for each year of assessment on the profits of any company accruing in, derived from, brought into, or received in Nigeria in respect of all kinds of income; that is, income derived from a trade, business, or investments. Thus, the tax holiday of companies in Nigeria is primarily on species of income having their source or deemed sourced within the country as well as on remittances.

[207] The Finance Act revised the Company Income Tax (CIT) Rates based on the revenue of companies, so as to provide tax relief to small- and medium-sized companies (SMEs). Small companies (with an annual turnover of less than NGN 25 million) are exempted from paying CIT subject to timely filing of CIT returns; medium companies (with NGN 25 million to NGN 100 million turnover) shall be subject to a CIT of 20%; and large companies (with more than NGN 100 million turnover) shall pay a standard CIT rate of 30%.

5.12.2 Dividends and Other Company Distributions

[208] In Nigeria, a company paying dividends to its shareholders is, first of all, obliged to pay tax on its profits at the companies tax rate before paying dividends to its shareholders. In a bid to eliminate elements of double taxation for companies, the Finance Act introduced exceptions to Excess Dividend Tax (EDT) Provisions of the Companies Income Tax Act; EDT is now only applicable to untaxed distributions other than profits specifically exempted from tax and franked investment income.

[209] As a general rule, any dividend or other company distribution, whether or not of a capital nature, made by a Nigerian company, is liable to a withholding tax at source of 10%. However, any dividend paid by a Nigerian company in the form of bonus/scrip share issues is not taxable in the hands of individual shareholders and is excluded from the profits of any other company that is a shareholder in such company.

Taxation of Non-Resident Companies

[210] The Finance Act introduced provisions to tax any foreign company that 'transmits, emits or receives signals, sounds, messages, images or data of any kind from cable, radio, electromagnetic systems or any other electronic or wireless apparatus to Nigeria in respect of any activity, including electronic commerce, application store, high frequency trading, electronic data storage, online adverts, participative network platform, online payments and so on, to the extent that the company has significant economic presence in Nigeria and profit can be attributable to such activity'.

[211] Also, the Finance Act amended the provisions of CITA to reflect that income earned by foreign companies from technical, management, consultancy or professional services that are remotely provided to a person resident in Nigeria would be subject to withholding tax deductions.

Tax Identification Number

[212] The Finance Act mandatorily requires all companies to provide a Tax Identification Number (TIN) as a precondition for opening or continued operations of an account with a bank or any other financial institution.

5.13 Double Taxation Relief Agreements

[213] In the last few years, double taxation agreements have been entered into by Nigeria with a number of countries. These agreements are entered into with a view to affording relief from double taxation in relation to taxes imposed on profits taxable in Nigeria and any taxes of similar character imposed by the laws of the country concerned.

[214] In Nigeria, the OECD model has served as the basis on which most of the current double taxation treaties (DTTs) with other countries have been formulated. The method of relief from double taxation under Nigeria's tax treaties is by way of a 'tax credit'. The mechanism of the tax credit is such that the tax payable in Nigeria on profits of a Nigerian company being remitted into the country is reduced by the amount of 'foreign tax' paid abroad. The converse position is equally true where an overseas company receives profits from Nigeria that have already been taxed in Nigeria.

[215] As at the date of this publication, officially gazetted Double Taxation Treaties have been concluded between Nigeria and the following countries:

- Belgium
- Canada
- China
- Czech Republic
- France
- Mauritius
- Netherlands
- Pakistan
- Philippines
- Romania
- United Kingdom
- South Africa
- South Korea
- Spain
- Sweden
- Italy.

[216] The treaties with South Korea and Sweden are still being ratified. Also, negotiations are in progress to conclude similar treaties with other countries.

6 THE REGULATORY FRAMEWORK FOR MERGERS AND ACQUISITIONS

[217] All the capital market laws regulating dealings in investments and securities in Nigeria are consolidated within the framework of the Investments and Securities Act, 2007 (ISA), which came into force from 25 June 2007 and repealed the erstwhile ISA of 1999. The ISA establishes the SEC, which acts as the apex regulatory body of the Nigerian Capital Market. As the apex regulator, it is saddled with the regulation of the Nigerian Capital Market to ensure the protection of investors, maintain fair, efficient and transparent market and reduction of systemic risk.

[218] Prior to the enactment of the Federal Competition and Consumer Protection Act 2018 ('FCCPA'), mergers and acquisitions in Nigeria were principally regulated by the ISA with the SEC having general regulatory oversight. However, the FCCPA has now repealed certain sections of the ISA as it relates to mergers and acquisitions.[2] The passage of the FCCPA also resulted in the introduction of a new regulatory framework for merger transactions in Nigeria. Currently, mergers and acquisitions in Nigeria are principally regulated by the FCCPA with the Federal Competition and Consumer Protection Commission ('FCCPC') exercising general regulatory oversight. The FCCPA establishes the FCCPC, which acts as the competition regulator vested with the powers to prevent and punish anti-competitive practices, regulates mergers and acquisitions, and promotes economic efficiency in Nigeria, among other functions.

[219] The Corporate Affairs Commission (CAC) established by the Companies and Allied Matters Act (CAMA) also plays a part in Mergers and Acquisitions. It is the responsibility of the CAC to receive corporate filings and to certify corporate resolutions and de-registration of any dissolved company that may occur in the merger process. Where a new company also emerges, it is the responsibility of the CAC to register such a company.

[220] The Nigerian Stock Exchange (NSE) plays a key role with regards to the reorganization of quoted public companies. Quoted companies are required to satisfy the listing rules on merger transactions.

[221] The Court of original jurisdiction for matters arising out of mergers and acquisitions is the Federal High Court, as it is empowered by the Constitution of the Federal Republic of Nigeria to handle matters with respect to companies' operation, management and regulation.

[2] Section 165 of the FCCPA repeals Sections 118–128 of the ISA (excluding Section 121 (1)(d) of the ISA).

6.1 Legal Responsibility of FCCPC in Mergers and Acquisitions

[222] Section 93(1) of the FCCPA provides that;

> Subject to the notification threshold to be determined from time to time as set out in this Part, a proposed merger shall not be implemented unless it has first been notified to and approved by the Commission.

6.2 Definition of Merger under the FCCPA

[223] By virtue of Section 92(1), a merger occurs when one or more undertakings directly or indirectly acquire or establish direct or indirect control over the whole or part of the business of another undertaking; and a merger can be achieved in any manner, including through the purchase or lease of the shares, interest or assets of the other undertaking in question, the amalgamation or other combination with the other undertaking in question, or a joint venture.

6.3 Scope of FCCPC-Regulated Transactions

[224] The FCCPC currently regulates all mergers and acquisitions in Nigeria. Under the FCCPA, mergers are categorized into two, namely, small mergers and large mergers. The scope of the FCCPA transcends the borders of Nigeria and particularly, the Act applies to conduct outside Nigeria by any person in relation to the acquisition of shares or other assets outside Nigeria resulting in the change of control of a business, part of a business or any asset of a business, in Nigeria. In essence, any merger between non-Nigerian entities that results in a change of control of a Nigerian business will come under the regulatory purview of FCCPC.

[225] The FCCPC released guidelines for notification of Foreign-to-Foreign mergers, '*Guidelines on Simplified Process for Foreign to Foreign Mergers with Nigerian Component*' in November 2019. The documentation requirements are less elaborate than that for local mergers. Key highlights of the Guidelines are as follows:

- Parties are to provide the FCCPC with a description of the merger. The description will be contained in three separate documents vis an executive summary providing details as to the parties, nature, activities and impact of the merger; a non-confidential summary of not more than five hundred words that would be published by the FCCPC; and an explanation as to why the merger qualifies for simple treatment by the FCCPC.
- The FCCPC is to be provided with comprehensive information of the parties to the merger such as the name of the undertaking, contact information, addresses within and outside Nigeria, details of representatives, evidence of a

power of attorney (where applicable), and the nature of the undertaking's business.

- Details of the merger, ownership and control are to be submitted with the application to the FCCPC. The information may, in part, be illustrated by the use of organization charts or diagrams to show the matrix of relationships, the structure of ownership and control of the undertakings before and after completion of the merger.
- Each of the undertakings concerned is to provide information on turnover in Nigeria in the last financial year. The FCCPC mandates that the financial information used for calculating the turnover of an undertaking shall include the undertaking's audited financial statements, for the end of the immediately preceding financial year to the notification.
- Information about Local Market Activities of the undertakings is to be provided. This may include a brief summary of the main subsidiaries active and/or brands, product names and/or trademarks used within Nigeria; an estimate of the total size of the market in terms of sales value (in Naira) and volume (in units); and innovations in products and/or services brought to the market over the last three years, products intended for the market over the next three years, as well as important intellectual property rights owned or controlled, or otherwise legitimately exercised under licence, franchise or similar arrangements.
- The Applicable Fees for Foreign-to-Foreign Merger Notifications are:
  (i) A merger with a combined turnover of NGN 1 billion and above shall attract a fee of NGN 3 million or 0.1% of the combined turnover, whichever is higher.
  (ii) A merger where target undertaking has a turnover of up to NGN 500 million and between N1 billion shall attract a fee of NGN 2 million.
- The expedited procedure fee is NGN 5 million to be paid in addition to the application fee. Under the expedited procedure, the Commission shall conclude its review and issue its decision within fifteen business days.

[226] The FCCPA is applicable to a body corporate or agency of the Government of the Federation or a body corporate or agency of a subdivision of the Federation if the body corporate or agency engages in commercial activities, or a body corporate in which a Government of the Federation or government of a State or a body corporate or agency of Government of the Federation or any State or Local Government has a controlling interest where such a body corporate engages in economic activities.

6.4 Exempted Transactions

[227] Section 92(3) of the FCCPA exempts credit institutions or other financial institutions or insurance companies, the normal activities of which include transactions and dealing in securities for their own account or for the account of others, holding on a temporary basis, securities which they have acquired in an undertaking with a view to reselling them, provided that they do not exercise voting rights in respect of those securities with a view to determining the competitive behaviour of that undertaking or provided that they exercise such voting rights only with a view to preparing the disposal of all or part of that undertaking or of its assets or the disposal of those securities.

[228] Control by an office-holder according to the laws of the Federation relating to liquidation, winding up, insolvency, cessation of payments, compositions or analogous proceedings are also exempted.

[229] Also, the provisions of the SEC regulation (which are still applicable by virtue of the Joint Advisory issued by the FCCPC and SEC) shall not apply to:

(a) holding companies acquiring shares solely for the purpose of investment and not for the purpose of using the shares by voting or otherwise to cause or attempt to cause substantial restraint of competition or tend to create a monopoly in any line of the business enterprise; or
(b) in a small merger, the merging entities shall not be required to notify the Commission of that merger but shall be required to inform the Commission at the conclusion of the merger.

[230] Notwithstanding the above, an acquisition in a private/unquoted public company with assets or turnover below NGN 500 million shall not be subject to the prior review and approval of the Commission.

6.5 Legal Responsibility of SEC in Mergers and Acquisitions

[231] Due to the introduction of a new regulatory framework for mergers and acquisitions in Nigeria, the previous extensive powers of SEC have been highly streamlined. The role of SEC in relation to mergers and acquisitions will be in the exercise of its primary function as the apex regulator of the Nigerian Capital Market. The regulatory powers of SEC will be restricted to determining whether all shareholders are fairly, equitably and similarly treated and given sufficient information regarding mergers by or involving public companies, as well as transactions involving a change of shareholding of capital market operators. The FCCPC is now to handle the anti-competitive effects of a transaction in a relevant market.

[232] Where any merger or acquisition involves a public company, the public company still has a duty to obtain the 'No Objection' of the SEC. Every public company undertaking a proposal, scheme, transaction, arrangement, or activity or issue of securities or offer for subscription or purchase of securities in relation to:

- the conversion of a public company or the reconstruction of its shares;
- a carve-out, spin-off, split-off or other forms of restructuring of its operations;
- the acquisition or disposal of assets which results in a significant change in the business direction or policy of a public company or any other listed entity

whether or not in relation to any proposal, scheme, transaction, arrangement or activity;

- shall obtain the No Objection of the SEC.

[233] Pursuant to the provisions of the ISA, the Commission is at liberty to make and amend rules and regulations applicable for the construction of the ISA.

[234] In the last decade, SEC adopted new rules and made amendments to the existing rules and regulations of the Commission, which have been duly reflected in the contents of this chapter.

Rule 230, Securities and Exchange Commission Rules (Exemptions)

[235] SEC – exempted transactions are:

(i) holding companies acquiring shares solely for the purpose of investment and not for the purpose of using the shares by voting or otherwise to cause or attempt to cause substantial restraint of competition or tend to create a monopoly in any line of the business enterprise;

(ii) transactions undertaken under authority given by any Federal Government agency vested with such statutory power.

6.6 Synergy Between the FCCPC and SEC

[236] It is pertinent to note that in compliance with the FCCPA, a Memorandum of Understanding on Regulatory Collaboration was executed between SEC and FCCPC to ensure the seamless operation of the mandates of both organizations. The FCCPC and SEC issued the *'Joint Advisory and Guidance on Mergers, Acquisitions and Other Business Combinations Notifications pursuant to the FCCPA'* ('Joint Advisory') in May 2019. The highlights of the Joint Advisory are as follows:

- All notifications or filings of pending or subsequent merger transactions will be reviewed under existing SEC regulations, guidelines and fees.
- All new notifications of mergers and requests for approval of mergers are to be filed at the FCCPC's office in Abuja or at the SEC/FCCPC Interim Joint Merger Review Desk in Abuja or Lagos.
- All fees are to be paid to the FCCPC.

[237] The import of this Joint Advisory is that both regulators will collectively review all notifications and filings, while the FCCPC is responsible for conveying the decision of such reviews. It is also safe to say that despite the enactment of the FCCPA, SEC's rules and regulations on mergers and acquisitions remain in force until the FCCPC issues a notice to the contrary.

[238] In addition to the above, the FCCPA provides that the Act is applicable to and binding on:

(i) All undertakings and commercial activities within, or having an effect within Nigeria.

(ii) A body corporate or agency of the Government of the Federation or a body corporate or agency of a subdivision of the Federation, if the body corporate or agency engages in commercial activities.
(iii) A body corporate in which a Government of the Federation or government of a State or a body corporate or agency of Government of the Federation or any State or Local Government has a controlling interest where such a body corporate engages in economic activities.
(iv) All commercial activities aimed at making a profit and geared towards the satisfaction of demand from the public.

6.7 Legal Requirements of the Companies and Allied Matters Act, 2020

Acquisition

a. Right of first **o**ffer and restrictions on the transfer of shares

CAMA 2020 imposes an obligation on shareholders in a company, who intend to sell their shares to make the first offer of the shares to the existing shareholders in that company before offering to a third party.

Also, a company must first obtain approval from its members before it can dispose of assets having values exceeding 50% of its total assets. Furthermore, a member acting alone or in conjunction with other members shall not sell more than 50% of the shares in a company to a third party except **if** the third party is willing to buy all the shares in the company and on the same terms.

Mergers

a. Power to Merge Associations

The CAMA 2020 empowers two or more associations under the act, with similar aims and objects to merge, subject to terms and conditions as may be prescribed by the Corporate Affairs Commission.

However, it is noteworthy that this provision does not conflict with any regulation made or may be made by the Federal Competition and Consumer Protection Commission with regards to mergers, rather it is complementary to the regulation by virtue of *Section 164 of Federal Competition and Consumer Protection Act* which provides that any provision of other legislations which is intended to also apply to matters within the powers of the FCCPC are to be interpreted as per the FCCPA.

Separate Meetings for Mergers of two or more Companies

Upon application by any of the companies to a merger, CAMA 2020 empowers the court to issue an order for a separate meeting of the companies. Members of the companies representing at least three-quarters in value of the share of members must be present in person or by proxy to vote and agree to the scheme at each of the separate meetings before the Court can sanction the same. Once the scheme has been sanctioned by the court, it becomes binding on all parties.

The repeal of the provisions of sections 118–128 of Investment and Securities Act by the Federal Competition and Consumer Protection Act left a vacuum in the regulatory framework for mergers in this regard, and this new CAMA provision for Mergers and Acquisitions has filled the vacuum.

7 STATUTORY INVOLVEMENT OF COURT SANCTIONS IN MERGERS AND ACQUISITIONS

[239] The SEC Rules require that companies proposing a merger, acquisition, or other forms of external restructuring shall:

(a) file with the Commission, a merger notification for evaluation;
(b) file an application in the Federal High Court seeking an order to convene a court-ordered meeting;
(c) following the resolution of the shareholders at the court-ordered meeting, the applicants shall file with the Commission a formal application for approval of the merger; and
(d) comply with post-approval requirements.

[240] Where all requirements have been fulfilled, the Commission shall inform the court, by a statement in writing whether the merger is approved, subject to conditions or prohibited. The court is required to sanction the scheme of arrangement.

[241] Upon approval by the Commission and the court order sanctioning the scheme, the applicant is required to file the following;

(a) a copy of the court order sanctioning the scheme within seven days of the court making the order;
(b) a copy of the newspaper publication of the court order;
(c) a statement of the actual cost of the scheme;
(e) a notification of the completion or otherwise of the exercise within three (3) months of the court's order; and
(f) summary reports of the scheme.

8 CATEGORIES AND THRESHOLDS OF MERGERS UNDER THE FCCPA

[242] The FCCPA makes mention of two categories of mergers namely:

(1) Small Merger: A merger with a value at or below the threshold stipulated by the Commission (FCCPC) by regulations. A party to a small merger is not required to notify the Commission of that merger unless the Commission requires it to do so, and the merger may be implemented without approval unless a party is required to notify the Commission. A party to a small merger may, however, voluntarily notify the Commission of the merger at any time.
(2) Large Merger: A merger with a value above the threshold stipulated by the Commission (FCCPC) by regulations. A party to a large merger shall notify the Commission of the merger in the prescribed manner and form. The parties to a large merger shall not implement the merger unless approved, with or without conditions, by the Commission.

[243] The FCCPA further provides that the Commission shall, by regulations, determine:

(a) a threshold of annual turnover for the purposes of determining the categories of mergers contemplated under the Act; and
(b) a method for the calculation of annual turnover to be applied in relation to the threshold determined.

[244] Pursuant to the Joint Advisory issued by the FCCPC and SEC, all merger reviews are to be done under existing SEC Regulations and Guidelines until further notice.

[245] As of July 2020, the FCCPC is yet to release regulations stipulating the thresholds for mergers, and as such the thresholds stipulated by the SEC are still applicable.

[246] The SEC Rules quantify the thresholds for a merger:

(a) The lower threshold for a small merger shall be below NGN 1 billion of either combined assets or turnover of the merging companies, the intermediate threshold shall be between NGN 1 billion and NGN 5 billion, while the upper threshold shall be above NGN 5 billion.
(b) Also, the determination of the threshold shall be by the combination of assets or turnover or the combination of both turnover and assets in Nigeria.

[247] These thresholds were created by the SEC to ensure its focus on transactions with significant economic impact. Any acquisition of shares or assets of a Company with assets or turnover of less than NGN 1 billion is deemed as a small merger, of which the parties are not required to notify the Commission unless the Commission requires it to do so, while all intermediate and large mergers, that is, a merger of parties with a combined turnover or assets of NGN 1 billion or more are required to be notified to the Commission.

[248] In determining the notification threshold, the sum of the combined assets or combined turnovers of the parties to the merger should be used. The notification requirement is not limited to public or quoted companies as it applies to all registered companies.

9 REGULATION OF TAKEOVER BIDS

[249] The ISA draws a clear distinction between 'mergers and acquisitions' and 'takeovers' and provides separate rules and different procedures for accomplishing each.

[250] In a public notice issued by the SEC, it was stated that the provisions and application of sections 131–151 of the Investments and Securities Act, 2007 remain unaffected by the enactment of the Federal Competition and Consumer Protection Act.

[251] The provisions relating to takeover bids as contained in sections 131–151 of the ISA may be summarized briefly as follows:

(1) A takeover bid is deemed to be made where any person who:
 (a) acquires shares, whether by a series of transactions over a period of time or not, which (taken together with shares held or acquired by persons acting in concert with him) carry 30% or more of the voting rights of a company; or
 (b) together with persons acting in concert with him, holds not less than 30% but not more than 50% of the voting rights and such person or any person acting in concert with him, acquires additional shares which increase his percentage of the voting rights, such person shall make a takeover offer to the holder of any class of equity share capital in which such person or any person acting in concert with him holds shares.

(2) A takeover bid cannot, however, be made in any case where a bid is dispatched:
 – to fewer than twenty shareholders, in order to purchase shares by way of separate agreements UNLESS it is dispatched to the holders of an aggregate of 51% of the issued and paid-up shares; or
 – to purchase shares in a company that has fewer than twenty shareholders.

(3) A takeover bid cannot legally be made in any case where the shares to be acquired under a bid are the shares of a private company.

(4) An application for 'authority to proceed' with a takeover bid must be made to the SEC. In this connection, the Commission may require the person making the bid to furnish it with such information as it considers necessary to enable it to make a decision on the application. The SEC may consult with such persons as it deems necessary to make a decision on an application.

(5) For the purpose of deciding whether or not to grant 'an authority to proceed' with a takeover bid, the SEC must have regard only to the likely effect of the takeover bid if successfully made:

(a) on the economy of Nigeria;
(b) on the policy of the federal government with respect to manpower and development, and if satisfied that none of the matters referred to in (a) and (b) above would be adversely affected, the SEC would grant an 'authority to proceed' with the proposed takeover bid, but if not so satisfied, it shall refuse to do so.

(6) A copy of any bid that is proposed must be duly signed and shall be lodged with the SEC who shall register the bid if satisfied that:
- the bid being an invitation to the public is embodied in a document that states the name and address of the offeror;
- the bid specifies the maximum number and other particulars of the shares proposed to be acquired during a period specified in the invitation;
- the bid has been approved by a resolution of the board of directors; and
- the bid specifies the terms on which those shares are proposed to be acquired.

(7) The directors of an offeree company are obliged to send a circular that may include an expert opinion to each shareholder of the company giving details and particulars of a takeover bid. Where a director is of the opinion that a bid is not advantageous to the shareholders of the offeree company or disagrees with any statement in a directors' circular, he or she is entitled to indicate his or her opinion or disagreement in the directors' circular stating the reasons for that opinion or disagreement. It is important to explain that a directors' circular must, among other things, include particulars of any payments made to an officer or former officer of the offeree company by way of 'compensation for loss of office'.

(8) A takeover bid may be for all or a part of a target company's shares.

(9) A number of provisions applicable to every takeover bid should be noted, including, for example, the following:
- shares deposited pursuant to the bid may be withdrawn by or on behalf of a shareholder in the offeree company at any time within ten days after the date of the takeover bid;
- shares deposited pursuant to the bid shall be taken up and paid for within fourteen days;
- if the terms of the bid are amended by increasing the consideration offered for the shares, the offeror shall pay the increased consideration to each shareholder whose shares are taken up pursuant to the bid, whether or not the shares have been taken up before the amendment;
- if the offeror intends to purchase shares in the offeree company in the market during the period of time within which shares may be deposited pursuant to the bid, the offeror shall so state in the bid.

(10) Where 90% of a takeover bid has been accepted, a dissenting shareholder may elect to transfer his or her shares to an offeror on the terms on which the offeror acquired the shares of the offeree who accepted the takeover bid or alternatively, to demand payment of the fair value of his or her shares.

[252] In 2017, SEC approved amendments to its Rules on Takeovers, such as its applicability and scope of enforcement:

1. Where any person, directly or indirectly:
   (a) acquires shares or an interest in shares, whether by a series of transactions over a period of time or not, which (taken together with shares held or acquired by persons acting in concert with him) carry 30% or more of the voting rights of a public company; or
   (b) together with persons acting in concert with him, holds not less than 30% but not more than 50% of the voting rights and such person or any person acting in concert with him acquires additional shares or an interest in shares or is interested in additional shares which increase his percentage of the voting rights of a public quoted company.

   Such person shall make a takeover bid to the holders of any class of equity share capital in the target company through an agent who shall be a registered Capital Market Operator.
2) A takeover bid shall not be made or required to be made:
   (a) to fewer than 20 shareholders representing 60% of the members of the target company or such other members as may be prescribed by the Commission from time to time;
   (b) where the shares to be acquired under the bid are shares in a private company save where such private company within the immediately preceding twelve months converted from a public quoted company to a private company;
   (c) where an ailing company undertakes a private placement approved by the Commission which results in the strategic investor acquiring more than 30% of the voting rights of the company;
   (d) an acquisition or holding of or entitlement to exercise or control the exercise of more than 30% voting shares of a company by an allotment made in accordance with a proposal, particulars of which were set out in a prospectus where:
      (i) the prospectus was the first prospectus for the initial public offer of voting shares issued by the company;
      (ii) the person who acquired the voting shares was a promoter in respect of the prospectus and the effect of the acquisition on the person's voting power in the company has been disclosed in the prospectus;
      (iii) the prospectus has been registered with the Commission;
   (e) upon conversion of convertible securities issued with the approval of shareholders in a general meeting;
   (f) where shares carrying 50% or more of the outstanding voting rights of the company are held directly or indirectly by one person;
   (g) where holders of shares carrying 50% or more of the outstanding voting rights of the company state in writing that they would not accept a mandatory bid.

10 ADDITIONAL REGULATORY REQUIREMENTS FOR MERGERS AND ACQUISITIONS IN SOME SPECIALIZED INDUSTRIES

[253] The FCCPA is the primary legislation on mergers and acquisitions in Nigeria. However, mergers and acquisitions involving undertakings in regulated industries are also subject to the provisions of the various sectoral legislation. These legislations require further approval to mergers from the regulators of these industries. These sector-specific laws operate in addition to the provisions of the FCCPA, ISA, the Companies and Allied Matters Act and the SEC Rules and Regulations.

10.1 Banking

[254] Where banking institutions are involved in mergers and acquisitions, there is a statutory obligation to obtain the prior and final approval of the Governor of the CBN before such arrangement is consummated.

[255] Section 7 of the Banks and Other Financial Institutions Act (BOFIA) provides that:

> except with the prior consent of the Governor, no bank shall enter into an agreement or arrangement:
>
> (a) which results in a change in the control of the bank;
> (b) for the sale, disposal or transfer howsoever, of the whole or any part of the business of the bank;
> (c) for the amalgamation or merger of the bank with any other person;
> (d) for the reconstruction of the bank; and
> (e) to employ a management agent or to transfer its business to any such agent.

[256] However, in addition to satisfying the provisions of BOFIA on mergers and acquisitions, banking institutions are still required to comply with the statutory requirements of the FCCPC in this regard. In other words, compliance with the provisions of BOFIA is only a part of the overall regulatory requirements by banks in a merger process.

[257] In 2005, the Central Bank of Nigeria issued Revised Procedures Manual for Processing Applications for Bank Mergers/Takeovers. The Manual provides explicitly, the allowable legal modes of consolidation by banks, which are mergers and takeovers; the stages for approval for mergers (three stages) and takeovers (two stages); timelines for completing the processing and conveying approvals; and the documentation required for the process.

10.2 Insurance

[258] The Insurance Act provides that no insurer shall amalgamate with, transfer to or acquire from any other insurer, any insurance business or part thereof, without the approval of the National Insurance Commission (NAICOM) or the sanction of the court. Part V of the Insurance Act goes on to prescribe the various procedural matters to be observed in consummating any mergers and acquisitions within the industry. However, these proceedings must be construed as being supplemental to the FCCPC regulatory proceedings on mergers and acquisitions.

10.3 Telecommunications

[259] The Nigerian Communications Act, supported by the NCC Competition Practices Regulations 2007, makes it mandatory that licenses issued by the Nigerian Communications Commission (NCC) to any company will require the NCC's prior consent to any share transfers that would result in a change of control or to arrangements (such as a merger) that would result in a license transferring to any entity other than the one to which the license was originally issued.

[260] They also provide further guidance on the standards and procedures which the Commission will apply in determining whether particular conduct (such as mergers) constitutes substantial lessening of competition in the telecommunications sector.

10.4 Electric Power

[261] The Electric Power Sector Reform Act, 2004 (EPSRA) established the Nigeria Electricity Regulatory Commission (NERC) as the regulator for the licensing and regulation of the generation, transmission, distribution and supply of electricity and as the enforcer of such matters as consumer rights and obligations. The NERC regulates both issuances of licenses and changes in status or control of licensees and has the power to decide whether or not to approve a merger or acquisition in the Nigerian power sector.

10.5 Health Services

[262] The National Health Insurance Scheme Operational Guidelines (revised in 2012) provides guidelines on mergers and acquisitions within the health sector.

[263] The Guidelines provide that no Health Maintenance Organisation (HMO) or Civil Society Organization (CSO) shall merge with, transfer to or receive from any other HMO its business or lives without the approval of the Scheme in writing.

[264] Also, no Mutual Health Associations (MHA) shall merge with, transfer to or receive from any other MHA its business or lives without the approval of the Scheme in writing. The Board of Trustees, however, shall retain the power to register more enrollees to the benefit of the MHA/organization.

10.6 Oil and Gas

[265] In 2014, the Department of Petroleum Resources issued 'Guidelines and Procedures For Obtaining Minister's Consent To The Assignment Of Interest In Oil And Gas Assets', which were made pursuant to specified provisions of the Petroleum Act (Cap. P10 LFN, 2004) and Oil Pipelines Act (Cap. O7 LFN, 2004).

[266] The guidelines stipulate that an application for a merger or acquisition involving a Publicly or Privately quoted Company shall be by way of a written application to the Director of Petroleum Resources requesting the Minister's consent containing a copy of the approvals, documents and rules governing such mergers and acquisitions in all the relevant approving jurisdiction.

11 STOCK EXCHANGE CONTROLS

[267] In acquisition and merger transactions involving companies quoted on The Nigerian Stock Exchange (NSE), the listing requirements of the NSE have to be observed, in addition to all other previously stated formalities. The Rule Book of the Nigerian Stock Exchange provides compulsory guidelines on Mergers and Takeovers.

11.1 Stock Exchange Listing Requirements on Takeovers and Mergers

[268] The NSE Listing Requirements as they relate to Takeovers and Mergers are reproduced below verbatim.

> A LISTED COMPANY IS REQUIRED TO SUBMIT TO THE EXCHANGE DRAFTS OF ALL CIRCULARS TO BE ISSUED BY THE COMPANY TO ITS SHAREHOLDERS
>
> (1) All documents of offer shall contain as a heading the words 'if you are in any doubt about this offer you should consult your stockbrokers, bank manager, solicitor, professional accountant or other professional adviser', and must contain the particulars specified in paragraphs 2 to 16 below, in addition to complying with the relevant provisions of the Companies Act.

(2) The date the document is despatched, the names and address of the offeror and if appropriate, the person or company making the offer on behalf of the offeror.

(3) Precise particulars of the securities for which the offer is made whether they will be transferred cum/ex any dividend or interest payment that may be declared, the total consideration payable for the purpose, the period within which and the method by which any cash consideration will be paid, how any securities issued will rank for dividends, capital and redemption and when and how the document of title will be issued and how, and where any such offer may be accepted.

The offer shall open for at least 21 days. In the event of a change in the terms of the offer which is subsequently declared unconditional, the offer shall remain open for at least 21 days from the time of the change in the terms.

(4) It must state all conditions attached to acceptances and in particular whether the offer is conditional upon acceptance being received in respect of a minimum number of securities and if that is so, that minimum number and the last date on which the offer can be made unconditional. No offer may be conditional upon the payment of compensation for loss of offer. If any such payment is proposed, full particulars must be given. A partial offer must be on a pro-rata basis and the reason for the failure to make a full offer given.

(5) A statement as to whether the offeror or its directors or any person acting in concert with the offeror has beneficial interest whether direct or indirect, in any of the securities for which the offer is made, giving full details or an appropriate negative statement.

Details, including dates and costs, must be given of any transactions in the securities of which the offer is made by any of those persons during the period commencing 12 months prior to the announcement of the offer and ending with the latest practicable date prior to the posting of the offer document or an appropriate negative statement made.

(6) A statement as to whether or not any securities acquired under the offer will be transferred to any other person together with the names of the parties to such agreement and particulars of all securities in the offeree company held by such person, or a statement that no such securities are held.

(7) A statement as to whether or not any agreement or arrangement exists between the offeror and any of the directors of the offeree company having connection with or dependence upon the offer, and full particulars of any such agreement.

(8) The intentions of the purchaser as regarding the employees of the company and the continuance of the business.

(9) Particulars of all documents required to be lodged for valid acceptance shall be returned within fourteen days of the closing date of the offer, if the proposed purchase is not completed.

(10) If the offer is for cash and is made on behalf of the offeror, the offer documents shall state what steps have been taken to ensure that the offer will be implemented if all the offerees accept.

(11) If the total emoluments receivable by the directors of the purchasing company or group will be varied after the acquisition, the offer document must contain full particulars of the variation, if there will be no variation a statement to that effect must be made.

(12) (i) If the offer is for the exchange of securities the offer document must state the nature and particulars of the offeror company's business, its net profit before tax and rate percent of dividends on the securities offered and the amount distributed for the past three years, any financial advantage expected to accrue to an acceptor, whether the issue of the new securities requires the passing of a resolution, the first dividend in which they will participate and particulars of all material changes in the offeror company since the date of the last available accounts;

(ii) the new securities are not to be identical in all respects with an existing listed security; all points of difference, full particulars of the voting rights attaching thereto and whether application for permission to deal therein and listing thereof has been or will be made to The Exchange must be stated.

The Memorandum and Articles of Association, audited accounts for the last five fiscal years of the offeror or company and all material con-tracts shall be made available for inspection at a place in Nigeria.

(13) If the offer contains no recommendations by the offeree company's directors, the offer document must state particulars of any known material change in the offeree company's financial position since the publication of the last balance sheet.

(14) If the offer document or any circular sent out in connection therewith, whether by or on behalf of the offeror company includes a recommendation by a financial adviser or other expert who is a member of The Exchange for or against acceptance of the offer, Council may require the document, unless issued by the expert in question to include a statement that the expert has given and has not withdrawn his written consent to the issue of the document and the inclusion therein of his recommendation in the form and context in which it is included therein.

(15) If the offer is recommended by the directors, the offer documents must state the directors' recommendation regarding acceptance, the number, description and amount of securities held by or on behalf of the directors of the offeree company in that company and in the offeror company and their intentions as regards acceptance and otherwise of such holdings as may be relevant and full particulars of any material change in the financial position prospects and audited accounts.

(16) The Exchange reserves the right to request for any other further or additional information.

12 AN OUTLINE OF PROCEDURAL FORMALITIES IN MERGERS AND ACQUISITIONS

12.1 Legal Due Diligence

12.1.1 Confidentiality and Non-Disclosure Agreement

[269] The first step in a merger or acquisition is the conclusion of a confidentiality agreement. Before a party allows even the most preliminary due diligence operation, it will typically require the execution of a confidentiality agreement. This agreement gives the necessary assurance that, even if the transaction falls through, confidential information will be protected. For ease of reference, **Appendix A** is an indicative draft of a Confidentiality and Non-disclosure Agreement.

12.1.2 Memorandum of Understanding

[270] If the parties have reached an agreement-in-principle on the basic terms of the transaction, they must decide whether or not to sign a memorandum of understanding (MOU). An MOU, also known as a letter of intent, is drawn up between the parties to describe the intention of the parties and the course of action proposed. The MOU provides a summary of the business transaction and comprises a record of the main points on which the parties hope to reach an agreement and record key concerns of the parties.

[271] An MOU is usually non-binding but creates a moral climate to discourage either party from seeking to renegotiate later what they thought had been agreed. It is desirable for the MOU to address matters such as exclusivity period of 'no-shop' solicitation of competing bids, costs and break fee arrangements to apportion parties' costs (already incurred on professional advisers, etc.) should the transaction be abandoned. **Appendix B** is an indicative draft MOU with Heads of Agreement.

12.1.3 Due Diligence

[272] Working in conjunction with other professional advisers, the lawyers will play a leading role in the due diligence investigation of the legal, financial, tax, operational and other aspects of the business to assure that the client is really 'getting what is bargained or is bargaining for'. Solicitors normally will be very involved in the due diligence investigation of their own client, gathering and producing information for the other side ensuring that any required remedial actions are promptly spotted and rectified to inform the other party of the potential risks and rewards of the transaction. A reciprocal due diligence investigation will then be conducted into the affairs of the other company.

[273] The due diligence exercise entails gathering the information necessary to verify the price the purchaser will agree to pay, drafting the Business Combination Agreement, drafting the Disclosure Letter, and planning the running of the business after completion of the investment or business combination arrangement.

[274] The solicitors will draw up the due diligence questionnaire, which initiates the due diligence process. The due diligence questionnaire sets out the areas to be addressed and provides a list of questions to be answered and documents to be made available for inspection. The seller and its team will need to track the information given to the purchaser and should endeavour to maintain an efficient indexing system, to ensure that the information is formally disclosed in the Disclosure Letter, and to rely on the fact that the information has been given to the other party if any warranty claims arise. **Appendix C** is an indicative Legal Due Diligence Checklist.

12.1.4 Data Room

[275] To facilitate the due diligence process, a Data Room will be established. All requisite documents and information will be indexed and made available in a Data Room for due diligence investigation and verification of a bidding party and its advisers. It is usual and desirable to establish Data Room rules as to the procedure, periods of access and procedure for generating issues for clarification and responses to them.

[276] It is not permitted to take any documents out of a Data Room. Therefore, in the course of legal due diligence and within the time limits afforded, it is important to elicit information as to whether any licences, contracts or agreements contain 'change in control' clauses, and to ascertain whether such requirements may be cured by prior applications for consents and approvals. **Appendix C1** is an indicative format for guidance in compiling synopses of due diligence findings. Depending on the volume of documents available for inspection, the Data Room may be established as either a virtual data room or physical data room.

12.1.5 Drafting and Negotiating Transactional Documents and Issues

[277] In addition to the aforementioned, solicitors in the designated role will be actively involved in the process of drafting, negotiating and coordinating the execution of the documents and the completion of all legal actions necessary to carry out the transaction, including:

- conduct of due diligence investigation;
- warranties and representations;
- indemnities;
- disclosure letter;
- Business Combination Agreement;

- advising on the scheduling of meetings of directors and shareholders that may be required;
- advising on securities law and industry-specific regulations;
- inputs into preparation of materials for submission to regulatory authorities;
- litigation audit;
- applications to court for orders to convene meetings;
- filing petitions for orders sanctioning schemes;
- obtaining requisite court sanction of the schemes; and
- inputs, as may be necessary, into press releases and other circulars for the avoidance of any misleading content.

12.1.6 Some Practical Issues

[278] The method of acquiring the entire share capital of a company varies according to the number of shareholders in the target company that may have to be bought out. If there are only a few holders – say two or three – the purchaser can deal with them personally. Thus, in the case of unquoted, wholly indigenous companies with few members, acquisitions should be easy, as relatively few governmental and other approvals would be required.

[279] In public quoted companies whose shares are widely held, it is not possible to deal personally with all shareholders, and it, therefore, becomes necessary to prepare some kind of document or circular to be sent to all shareholders informing them of the terms of a merger or acquisition offer. These circulars need careful preparation.

[280] In the implementation of mergers and acquisitions, the procedure that has been generally mentioned as being desirable to be followed whether by those making offers or by the directors of target companies in receiving them may be summarized as follows:

(1) It is generally advisable that an offer (or an approach with a view to an offer) should be made in the first instance to the board of directors of the company for whose shares such an offer or approach is being made. Although the offeror is seeking to make a bargain with the shareholders, their board is normally the best channel of approach and also the shareholders' best source of advice.

(2) When talks which may lead to an offer are proceeding, it is important to do everything possible to maintain secrecy in order to avoid a disturbance in the normal price level of shares until the relevant information can simultaneously be made available to all shareholders. In particular, directors, or others who have close associations with them, should avoid any dealings in the shares that are likely to be affected ('insider dealing') and should exercise great care in connection with any transactions that may have been initiated but not completed when the talks begin.

(3) At the preliminary stages of discussions, it is important to make due diligence enquiries as to the existing business cultures and reward systems of

the target company. The analysis will minimize likely objections to the exercise from the management and staff of the target company as well as take into account the feelings and fears of the shareholders of the target company. Discreet approaches are made by the chief executives of both companies to carry along their staff trade union leaders with the merger's prospects, without necessarily divulging any matters that should still remain confidential to avoid premature information leaks. The aftermath of a merger usually necessitates a reorganization or rationalization of the board composition. Therefore, some advance planning is directed towards probable means of assuaging egos ruffled by the resultant merger – in particular, of the Chairman who loses his or her status in the resultant merger.

(4) It is usually unwise for a board to make any public announcement until it is reasonably certain that an offer will, in fact, be forthcoming, but once this stage in the negotiations has been reached, an announcement should be made with the minimum of delay. A joint announcement, in which the board of the offeree company may always reserve its position, is usually desirable.

(5) All announcements concerning 'offers' should, whenever possible, be made both through the press and by circular. A press announcement is normally the quickest way of making information generally available, which should, whenever possible, be confirmed by circular. However, the dissemination of information should not be delayed while a circular is being prepared. Care should be taken to ensure that any communication is made with the prior approval of the regulatory authorities.

(6) If a board decides to recommend that an offer should not be accepted, the offeror is still free to communicate directly with the shareholders, and in such a case the board should be ready to facilitate this direct approach (at the expense of the offeror) while at the same time explaining to its shareholders why it does not recommend the offer.

(7) Shareholders who are directors or who have a close association with the board have a duty, if they contemplate the sale of an effective controlling interest, to consider carefully whether the sale of their interest could affect the position of other shareholders, and whether in consequence, they ought to arrange for all other shareholders to be given an equivalent opportunity to sell.

(8) Where there has been no time to make formal offers to shareholders, an offeror who has previously publicly made his or her intentions to acquire shares known and who subsequently acquires effective control by buying, in the market or otherwise, should without delay revise his existing offer or make a formal offer to all uncommitted shareholders at a fair price having regard to the prices paid in the market. Purchases of some of the shares of any particular class, whether made through the market or otherwise, should not be made with special conditions attached that are not available to all shareholders of that class.

(9) An offeror who subsequently raises his or her offer price should always make arrangements for all shareholders who have previously accepted the offer to receive the revised higher price.

(10) An offeror declaring an offer unconditional should put shareholders who are then still uncommitted in the best position to decide their further action, by disclosing immediately the number of shares he has acquired by that time; the offer should then be kept open for a reasonable time to allow those uncommitted shareholders who may decide to accept to do so.

12.2 Branding/Marketing of the Newly Created or Surviving Entity: Preliminary Legal Issues

12.2.1 Corporate Affairs Commission and Trade Marks Office

[281] If it is proposed to adopt a new operative name for the new entity created, it is desirable as an initial step to propose two alternative names to the Solicitor. The Solicitor conducts an Availability Check at the Corporate Affairs Commission (CAC) on whether the name is available and identifies other prior registered names that may be similar enough to affect the distinctiveness in subsequent brand marketing.

[282] Search enquiries are conducted simultaneously by Solicitor at the Trade Marks Office to check availability of a proposed name for registration as a service mark.

[283] Immediately after the solicitors ascertain the name that is clear at both the CAC and the Trade Marks Office, the name should be filed for registration at the Trade Marks Office and effectively reserved for registration at the CAC. Such name would then be proposed for clearance.

[284] This preliminary due diligence helps to avoid a challenge to use of the name after expending a lot of money on the advertising campaign to introduce the new brand.

13 COMMON TYPES OF MERGERS AND BUSINESS COMBINATIONS

[285] The earliest recorded corporate merger and acquisition (M&A) transactions in Nigeria were in the mid-1980s. Initially, the larger and more prominent ones tended to be 'family affairs' and involved combinations between closely related companies.

[286] Since 2004, Nigerians have now generally become familiar with the M&A concept and terminology. In order to strengthen the financial industry for the avoidance of systemic failures, the Central Bank of Nigeria (CBN) imposed a deadline period within which the then-existing eighty-four banks had to undergo massive increases in their capital base to a stipulated minimum amount and, in lieu, to forfeit their banking licence. The quantum leap in capital base requirement imposed the necessity for public share offers and mergers and consolidation within the banking industry. After a frenzy of M&A activities within the industry, there were twenty-three surviving banks as of 2007. In 2005, the National Insurance Commission imposed similar obligations on operators in the insurance industry to shore up their capital base by a specific deadline date, and this attracted another flurry of M & A activities. Thereafter, the CBN set December 2013 as the deadline date for mortgage finance institutions to shore up their capital base and this attracted yet another flurry of M&A activities.

[287] More recently, the risk averse posture of local banks to venture capital has provided a growing market for private equity M&A activities. In general, private equity investments in a company are a demonstration of faith in the management team of the target company to deliver on the business plan and project cash flow forecast. The average tenure of private equity before they exit and recoup their investments is 5-7 years. On the other hand, prudential guidelines of the Central Bank require banks to secure loan facilities with adequate collaterals, and deposit banks generally limit their exposures to 3-5 years. Some of the recent mergers and acquisitions in the banking industry include the merger of Diamond Bank Plc. and Access Bank Plc., as well as the acquisition by Polaris Bank Limited of Skye Bank Plc. In the manufacturing sector, a notable transaction is the acquisition by the Coca-Cola Company of CHI Limited.

[288] By and large, transactions in the market have been driven by regulatory implications. Typically, the acquisition buy-in objective is to acquire an interest in a company which owns a vital non-transferable operating licence or permit. For illustration purposes, some types of business combinations are set out below.

13.1 Horizontal Merger

[289] This is the combination of enterprises in similar lines of business, as exemplified in the regulator-inspired mergers of banks, insurance companies and mortgage institutions. An indicative outline for Horizontal Scheme of Merger is set out in **Appendix D.**

13.2 'Buy-In' Acquisition by Strategic Core Investors

13.2.1 Urban Development Bank of Nigeria Plc. ('UDBN') Turnaround Project

CHECKLIST OF LEGAL & TRANSACTIONAL STEPS

13.3 Background

[290] In 1992, Federal Government of Nigeria ('FGN') played a significant catalytic role in the setting up of the Urban Development Bank of Nigeria ('UDBN') to serve as a Development Finance Institution in the infrastructure and urban development corridor. The initial share capital of UDBN was subscribed to by the Federal Government (20 percent), State Governments, collectively (20 percent), Local Governments, collectively (40 percent) Nigeria Labour Congress (10 percent), and 10 percent shareholding stake reserved for Nigerian individuals. FGN paid for the initial subscriptions of all the shareholders except the stake reserved for Nigerian individuals which nobody was interested in taking even up to fourteen years later.

[291] UDBN was effectively run as a government department, and its overheads and operational costs were funded from subventions and loans from the FGN. By 2006, UDBN had become significantly indebted to FGN for the long-term loans of an aggregate principal amount of NGN 751.5 million issued to the bank via the Ministry of Finance Incorporated ('MOFI'). These loans now constituted a major debt obligation which was unserviceable, with clear prospects that more loans would still be required to keep the bank in operation. FGN was considering putting a stop to the continuous financial drain, and without any visible impacts as a financial intermediary in the infrastructure and urban development areas. At the crucial period of FGN consideration about liquidation of the bank, Investor Ltd. emerged as a 'White Knight' serving the purpose of an investment vehicle for mobilizing equity investment into UDBN for the change of control and turnaround transaction. Investor Ltd. was established as a special purpose vehicle, and the prized asset in the debt-laden bank was its special banking licence.

13.3.1 Mechanics of Acquisition

(i) Credit Line investment by Investor Ltd. Investor Ltd. purchases UDBN's debts from MOFI at pre-negotiated payment consideration of NGN xxx million;

(ii) **Loan Novation Agreement** substitutes Investor Ltd., in place of UDBN, as Loan Obligor to MOFI/FGN;

(iii) **Issue and Subscription Agreement** whereby UDBN repackages Debt assumed by Investor Ltd. as 751.5 million newly issued common stock equity designated as newly created Class 'AA' ordinary shares;

(iv) MOFI and Investor Ltd. execute **Debt Acquisition Agreement.**

(v) 800 million *initial* shares of UDBN is designated as Class 'A' ordinary shares.

(vi) 80 million Class 'A' ordinary shares is allotted to the Nigerian Managing Partner of Investor Ltd. at pre-negotiated payment consideration of NGN xxx million;

(vii) **Shareholders' Agreement** establishes the respective rights and obligations of all Shareholders of UDBN.

13.3.2 Outline of Corporate Actions Undertaken

- **UDBN Shareholders' Resolutions:**
  - (a) to approve the **Loan Novation Agreement** and the repackaging of the Debt assumed by Investor Ltd. as 751.5 Million Class 'AA' Ordinary Shares of UDBN;
  - (b) to approve the **Issue and Subscription Agreement**;
  - (c) to approve the allotment of 80 million Class 'A' ordinary shares in the *initial* share capital of UDBN to the Nigerian Managing Partner of Investor Ltd.
  - (d) to adopt New Memorandum and Articles of Association, viz. Charter and By-Laws;
  - (e) to authorize Increase in Share Capital and Share Restructuring for capacity to absorb new shares;
  - (f) to classify the shares issued in the *initial* capital as Class 'A' ordinary shares and the newly issued shares as Class 'AA' ordinary shares;
  - (g) to approve appointments to Managing Board of Directors;
  - (h) to adopt Corporate Governance Policy;
  - (i) to approve Board Structure;
  - (j) to approve the formal representative bodies of the *initial* Shareholders;
  - (k) to approve re-branding of UDBN as The Infrastructure Bank of Nigeria Plc;
  - (l) to ratify all prior actions of the Federal Government of Nigeria in respect of the UDBN turnaround transaction and commit to taking all necessary corporate steps to implement the transaction.
- **Investor Ltd. Shareholders' Resolutions**
  - (a) Investor Ltd. Board Approval to enter into Debt Acquisition Agreement with MOFI
  - (b) Investor Ltd. Board Resolution to invest in 751.5 million Class 'AA' Ordinary Shares of UDBN;
- **Transaction Documents**
  - Tripartite **Loan Novation Agreement** between MOFI/UDBN/ Investor Ltd.;
  - **Debt Acquisition Agreement** between MOFI/ Investor Ltd.;
  - **Issue and Subscription Agreement** between Investor Ltd./UDBN;
  - New Memorandum and Articles of Association;
  - Corporate Governance Policy for UDBN;
  - Shareholders Agreement amongst all the shareholders

Investor Ltd. became the core investor in UDBN, and Investor Ltd. shares are directly – linked to the bank's fortunes since that is the sole investment purpose of the special purpose vehicle. The main source of finance for the SPV was local bank equity investment, with other shareholders. Soon thereafter, the Central Bank directed all banks to divest from non-core banking business and investments. By liberal interpretation, the SPV did not qualify as banking business. With growing prospects of capital appreciation, Investor Ltd. was able to attract new equity shareholders, to take over the bank equity investor's pioneering stake.

13.4 ASSET MANAGEMENT COMPANY OF NIGERIA ('AMCON') – DIVESTMENTS

13.4.1 Background

[292] In response to the 2008/2009 Nigerian financial crisis, the Central Bank of Nigeria ('CBN') took a number of measures towards restoring the stability of the banking sector. A key feature of CBN's strategy was to promote the establishment of the Asset Management Company of Nigeria ('AMCON'), in 2010. AMCON was set up as a resolution vehicle to purchase Eligible Banking Assets ('EBAs') of Deposit Money Banks, and subsequently recapitalized 8 CBN – intervened banks.

[293] In August 2011, AMCON was invited by the Nigerian Deposit Insurance Corporation ('NDIC') to capitalize 3 Bridge Banks the NDIC had created, namely Enterprise Bank Limited, Mainstreet Bank Limited and Keystone Bank Limited (Collectively 'the AMCON Banks').

[294] The non-performing loans of some companies with Eligible Financial Institutions ('EFI') were also purchased by AMCON at various phases of EBA purchases. The settlement sums were restructured into equity investments which AMCON now owned.

[295] Since the last quarter of 2013, AMCON embarked on the divestment of its equity shareholding in the bridge banks and companies. The Proprietary Portfolio Department (PPD) is set up to manage the divestment of AMCON's stake from companies wherein the Corporation holds equity. The department co-ordinates the process and ensures that divestment of equity is carried out within the scheduled timelines.

[296] The AMCON Act was amended in 2015 and subsequently in 2019, with a view to increase the powers of AMCON to ensure the proper enforcement of the Act, accessibility to all relevant information and recovery of debt from debtors.

Transaction Dynamics

- AMCON advertises Requests for Proposals ('RFP') for Legal Advisers and Financial Advisers to advise on the transactions.
- The selected transaction advisers issue international tenders for Requests For Proposals ('RFP') from interested investors.
- The bidders are issued with Information Memoranda on the enterprise and given the opportunity to conduct their due diligence.
- Bidders are selected on the basis of the pricing, and Post-Acquisition Plans ('PAP') submitted by them.

13.5 MANAGEMENT BUY-OUTS

[297] In a management buyout, the managers of a business become its owners or core shareholders. However, the situation is normally complicated because the managers usually have insufficient funds to buy the company outright and therefore need a third party to finance the deal.

[298] This finance usually comes in the form of bank loans, but more recently, private equity and venture capital funds are perceived to be more dominantly involved. However, the providers of finance will wish to take adequate collateral security cover and also retain a stake in the target company, as preference shareholders, to give them a potential reward that takes into account their perceived risk. Unlike what obtains in most other jurisdictions, the current company laws of Nigeria make it mandatory for all classes of shareholders, including preference shareholders, who are in fact creditors, to receive notices and to attend and vote at all company meetings. Therefore, the preference shareholder is within easy reach of monitoring the company's activities.

13.5.1 Background to the Current Upsurge in Management Buy-Outs

[299] Sequel to the 2008/2009 Nigerian financial crisis, the Central Bank took a number of palliative measures towards restoring confidence in the financial sector. Notably, the CBN observed that the deposit banks had become progressively distracted from their core business of banking. Banks had established Subsidiary companies and investments in diverse businesses, including insurance (to insure bank customers and all collateral securities held by the banks), mortgage finance companies, and courier companies (to facilitate mail deliveries to nationwide branch networks). By 2012, the CBN directed the banks to divest from all companies and investments outside of the core banking business. In the course of the business hive-offs, a few instances of Management Buy-Outs have occurred.

Transaction Dynamics

1. In anticipation of the imminent sale/hive-off of its subsidiaries, the Bank as a beneficial holding company undertook a review of the subsidiaries. Thereafter, staff rationalization and other steps were undertaken to make the subsidiaries attractive to prospective acquisition bidders.
2. The 'keyman employees' of the Target company's management constituted themselves into a Management Buyout Team ('MBO team'), and approached the Bank to afford them the opportunity to participate in the acquisition bids for the target company.
3. The target company operates in a specialized business sector and has a reasonably good reputation and market share.
4. Invitations for Expressions of Interest ('EOI') were circulated by the Bank to prospective bidders, which included the MBO team.

5. The MBO team was able to attract the interest of Private Equity funding. Consequently, a joint venture company was registered in Mauritius, with the fund provider and the MBO team as the beneficial shareholders. The Loan Agreement, Shareholders' Agreement and other agreements were governed by the Laws of England, as the funding was coming from abroad. As the loan is being retired in a phased manner, the MBO team would gradually buy the shares held by the fund provider in the Joint Venture Company ('JVC'), over a five-year period.
6. The JVC participated in the acquisition bid for the Target company with other competitors and won.
7. Consequently, a Share Sale and Purchase Agreement ('SSPA') was executed between the Bank and the JVC.

14 ACQUISITIONS THROUGH PRIVATIZATION OF GOVERNMENT EQUITY DIVESTMENTS

14.1 Legal Framework

[300] The legal basis for privatization in Nigeria is the Public Enterprises (Privatization and Commercialization) Act Cap. P38 Laws of the Federation of Nigeria 2004 (the 'Privatisation Act'). The Privatisation Act establishes the National Council on Privatisation ('NCP') to determine political, economic and social objectives for privatization and commercialization of Public Enterprises (PEs).

[301] NCP approves policy and decisions in privatization and commercialization of PEs. The Privatisation Act also established the Bureau of Public Enterprises ('BPE') as a secretariat to NCP and the body that implements NCP policy and decisions. The NCP supervises the activities of the BPE and issues directions on the implementation of the privatization and commercialization programme.

[302] In setting the stage for the current and ongoing phases of the privatization programme, diverse laws have been enacted to prohibit and repeal erstwhile legislation creating government monopolies in such areas as mining, petroleum, telecommunications, energy, electricity and other infrastructural facilities.

[303] Full or partial privatization can be consummated through any or a combination of the following methods.

* Offer for sale to:

(a) the Nigerian public, in general, through the Stock Exchange; and
(b) core investor(s) by direct tender(s) to the BPE as a vendor.

[304] It should be noted that although both the (a) and (b) offers are based on the information memoranda compiled by the professional parties/consultants assigned by BPE, as a vendor to the transaction, the shares on offer to the core investor(s) tend to attract a higher premium in view of the privileges attached to the controlling stakes.

[305] Save for the foregoing, the shares in a privatized enterprise subsequently rank *pari passu* in the capital of the enterprise.

14.2 Core Investor Selection Process

[306] The selection of core investors is made in an open, transparent, fair and competitive bidding process designed to ensure that only the most qualified bidder is chosen

[307] The NCP has approved that transactions will follow the process outlined below. It is clear that not all transactions can be exactly alike and slight variations to the approved processes will be inevitable in view of the particular nature of the enterprise, local and international market conditions, the level of investor appetite, policy considerations and, most importantly, the advice of the transactions advisers who will be required to structure and implement a privatization transaction strategy in line with international best practice. In cases where there is a need to vary the standard process to be followed, this variation will be considered and approved by the NCP and will then be communicated to all bidders as early as possible in the process and certainly before the actual bidding process commences.

[308] An outline of the typical transactions process is as follows.

14.3 Advertisement for Expressions of Interest (EOI)

[309] Prospective Core/Strategic Investors express their interest in response to an advertisement, which is usually placed in local and international media and a period of not less than thirty days given for responses. For the very small transactions, where international investor interest is unlikely, the focus of advertisements will be on local media.

14.4 Submission of Expressions of Interest

[310] All interested investors must abide by an advertised requirement, such as submission deadline, reporting structure, etc.

14.5 Evaluation of EOIs

[311] The evaluation is a pre-qualification exercise for determining which of the applicants are qualified to proceed to the next stage. The non-qualified applicants are promptly informed of their non-qualification, while the qualified ones are required to pay the registration fees specified in the advertisement in order to proceed to the next stage. It is at this stage that BPE and its advisers will commence the process of conducting due diligence on the prospective core investor. At this stage, only outline information is available on the bidding consortium, but as the process progresses and once technical bids are submitted (*see* below) more detailed investigations will be conducted. However, it is important to emphasize that such diligence is a continuous process that commences once EOIs are received until the final shortlist of pre-qualified investors is drawn up.

14.6 Bidding Documents

[312] The bidding documents lay down the ground rules for the transaction. The documents include a detailed outline of the bidding procedure, the Information Memorandum, which provides background information on the enterprise, the proposed contracts and other relevant bidding documents.

14.7 Due Diligence Exercise

[313] This is the Data Room process where prospective core investors have access to relevant information and documents of the enterprise being privatized. The Data Room will be open for a minimum period of four weeks during which the prospective core investors are expected to carry out a comprehensive due diligence of the company, including meetings with the management of the enterprise/BPE/Privatization Advisers and visiting field sites (where applicable).

[314] In addition, BPE responds to requests for information and addresses concerns and questions the bidders may have about the proposed transaction.

14.8 Submission of Bids

[315] Once bidders have had an opportunity to fully scrutinize the enterprise, they are invited to submit technical and financial bids (in separate sealed envelopes), as well as a bid bond in an amount to be set from time to time by the NCP and the level of which is usually determined on the basis of the size of the transaction. The bonds will be callable in the event that a prospective bidder defaults in its obligations to NCP. The bonds have 180 days' tenure.

[316] All late bids should be rejected and returned unopened.

14.9 Evaluation of Technical Bids

[317] An evaluation team is constituted comprised of members of the NCP/BPE and the transactions advisers. The prospective core investors whose technical proposals meet the minimum scores are qualified to proceed to the next stage, while those below will be declared unqualified and their financial proposals returned unopened.

14.10 Financial Bidding

[318] NCP has approved that, where feasible, the price will be the single determining variable for selection of the bidder to purchase government's equity in any particular public enterprise. Accordingly, once the technical bids have been evaluated, all those bidders that have been assessed to be technically qualified proceed to the financial bidding round when financial proposals are opened.

[319] Prior to opening the financial proposals, bidders submit their confirmation that their financial bids will be unconditional and will remain valid for a set period, usually 180 days, from the date of the bid opening. Next, the sealed financial bids, which had at an earlier stage been submitted in separate envelopes together with the technical bids, are opened in public. This opening will usually be televised live and will always take place in the presence of all bidders, the international diplomatic community, representatives from print and broadcast media and members of the general public that choose to attend.

[320] NCP also reserves the right to invite one or more additional round of bidding after the public announcement of the originally submitted bid. The decision to do this will be made well before the bidding process starts and will be announced clearly in the bidding documents sent to all bidders. This will ensure that the right to call for an additional bidding round is not exercised with a view to favouring any particular bidder.

[321] The additional bidding round will take place on the same date and at the same venue as the opening of the initial financial bids, and will also be televised live and take place in the presence of all bidders and the general public.

[322] The process of bid revision takes place in the open. Bidders are given a period of time, typically thirty minutes, within which to consider their revised proposals. Bidders are escorted to open but partitioned compartments where they may huddle and discuss their revised bids. However, during the process of considering the revised bids, consultations between bidding consortia are not allowed. Any such consultations may result in the disqualification of the offending party.

[323] Revised bids are indicated on pre-printed forms, signed by an authorized representative of the bidding consortium and sealed in an envelope for submission in public to NCP/BPE, whereupon the revised bids will be opened and announced in public and made available for review by the public.

[324] Bidders are reminded that revised bids must be given with the full authority of each bidding consortium. Bidders will have been advised beforehand that the key decision makers within their consortia should be present for the additional bidding round and should provide a written Power of Attorney confirming their authority to submit revised bids on behalf of the entire consortium.

[325] Downward adjustments of the bids quoted in the first round are not allowed. Bidders may, therefore, either waive their right to increase their bids from those quoted in the previous rounds or elect to increase them. In the event that they waive their rights, their bid in the first round shall remain applicable.

[326] All financial bids submitted in the second and any other subsequent rounds must also be provided free of any and all conditions.

[327] The bidder offering the highest price will be deemed as the 'Preferred Bidder' and the bidder offering the next highest price as the 'Reserve Bidder'. No price negotiations are permitted after the announcement of the Preferred Bidder.

14.11 Signing of Final Documents

[328] Discussions with the Preferred Bid on the outstanding terms of the contracts commence immediately after the announcement of the Preferred Bidder. As the proposed contracts were sent to all bidders as part of the bidding documents, there is usually little to negotiate, and major changes to the contract are not entertained by NCP. Generally, details of all the final transactions documents must be agreed within ten working days of the date of the financial bid opening. In the event that such discussions break down, NCP is free to commence discussions with the Reserve Bidder.

14.12 Financial Closure

[329] Typically, upon signing of final documents, the Preferred Bidder will be required to pay the purchase consideration within a short period. In certain cases, usually, where the transaction is large, the Preferred Bidder will be required to pay a deposit, usually of around 10% of the purchase consideration, immediately and then the balance within a predefined period of time. Generally, the period within which the payment of purchase consideration is required will tend to depend on the size of the transaction, outline valuation of the enterprise and the advice of the transactions advisers who will take cognizance of conditions in the local and international money and capital markets to determine an appropriate period that is fair to the Preferred Bidder. The period set will have been communicated to all bidders with the bidding documents.

[330] In the event that the Preferred bidder is unable to pay within the stipulated period, the NCP will seek to reach financial closure with the Reserve Bidders. If discussions with the Reserve Bidder also fail, or if the Reserve Bidder is equally unable to raise the required funds, the transaction is deemed to have failed.

[331] In cases where there is only one bidder remaining in the race, and that bidder fails to pay within the designated period, the NCP reserves the right to extend the payment period. The length of the extension should not be too long and will be determined upon the advice of the transaction advisers. The bidder will also be required to pay the penalty by way of a charge based on a default interest rate above the relevant Treasury bill rate quoted by the Central Bank of Nigeria or above LIBOR. This rate shall be applicable from the commencement date of the extension until the date of receipt of the payment.

14.13 Transfer of Management Control

[332] During the interim period, from the time the Share Sale Agreement is signed and full purchase consideration is paid, and upon which management control is ceded to the Preferred Bidder, an Interim Management Board will be put in place to run the enterprise, in order to preserve the value of the Enterprise.

[333] Upon the payment of the purchase of consideration, control will be transferred to the Core/Strategic Investor, and the shareholders would constitute a new Board of Directors.

15 ANTITRUST/COMPETITION ISSUES

[334] Whenever required to consider a merger, the Federal Competition and Consumer Protection Commission shall:

(a) initially determine whether or not the merger is likely to substantially prevent or lessen competition, by assessing the factors set out in section 94(2) of the FCCPA;
(b) if it appears that the merger is likely to substantially prevent or lessen competition, then determine:
   (i) whether or not the merger is likely to result in any technological efficiency or other pro-competitive gains that will be greater than, and offset, the effects of any prevention or lessening of competition, that may result or is likely to result from the merger, and would not likely be obtained if the merger is prevented; and
   (ii) whether the merger can or cannot be justified on substantial public interest grounds by assessing the factors set out in section 94(3) of the FCCPA.

(c) otherwise, determine whether the merger can or cannot be justified on substantial public interest grounds by assessing the factors set out in section 94(3) of the FCCPA.

[335] When determining whether or not a merger or a proposed merger is likely to substantially prevent or lessen competition, the Commission shall assess the strength of competition in the relevant market and the probability that the undertakings, in the market after the merger, will behave competitively or cooperatively, taking into account any factor that is relevant to competition in that market, including:

(a) the actual and potential level of import competition in the market;
(b) the ease of entry into the market, including tariff and regulatory barriers;
(c) the level and trends of concentration and history of collusion in the market;
(d) the degree of countervailing power in the market;
(e) the dynamic characteristics of the market, including growth, innovation, and product differentiation;
(f) the nature and extent of vertical integration in the market;
(g) the likelihood that the business or part of the business of a party to the merger or proposed merger has failed or is likely to fail; and
(h) the likelihood that the merger will result in the removal of an effective competitor.

[336] When determining whether a merger can or cannot be justified on public interest grounds, the Commission shall consider the effect that the merger will have on:

(a) a particular industrial sector or region;
(b) employment;
(c) the ability of small- and medium-scale enterprises to become competitive; and
(d) the ability of national industries to compete in international markets.

15.1 Small Merger: Discretions in Notification and Implementation

[337] In a small merger, the merging entities shall not be required to notify the FCCPC of that merger unless the FCCPC requires it to do so.

[338] A party to a small merger:

(a) is not required to notify the Commission of that merger unless the Commission requires it to do so;
(b) may implement the merger without approval unless required to notify the Commission; and

(c) when required to notify the Commission of the merger, shall forward the same documents as those required for a merger notification.

[339] A party to a small merger may voluntarily notify the Commission of the merger at any time.

[340] Within six months after a small merger has commenced implementation, the Commission may require the parties to the merger to notify the Commission of the merger in the prescribed manner and form if, in the opinion of the Commission, having regard to the provisions of section 94 of FCCPA, the merger:

(a) may substantially prevent or lessen competition; or
(b) cannot be justified on public interest grounds.

[341] A party to a merger required to notify the Commission of a merger pursuant to section 95(5) of FCCPA shall take no further steps to implement the merger until the merger has been approved or conditionally approved.

[342] Within twenty working days after all parties to a small merger have fulfilled all their notification requirements in the prescribed manner and form, the Commission:

(a) may extend the period in which it has to consider the proposed merger by a single period not exceeding forty days and, in that case, must issue an extension certificate to any party who notified it of the merger; or
(b) after having considered the merger in terms of section 94 of FCCPA, shall notify the parties in the prescribed form of:
    (i) its approval of the merger;
    (ii) approval of the merger subject to any conditions;
    (iii) the prohibition of the implementation of the merger, if it has not been implemented; or
    (iv) if already implemented, a declaration that the merger is prohibited.

[343] The SEC Rules require that companies proposing a merger, acquisition, or other forms of external restructuring shall:

(a) file with the Commission, a merger notification for evaluation;
(b) file an application in the Federal High Court seeking an order to convene a court-ordered meeting;
(c) following the resolution of the shareholders at the court-ordered meeting, the applicants shall file with the Commission a formal application for approval of the merger; and
(d) comply with post-approval requirements.

[344] Where all requirements have been fulfilled, the Commission shall inform the court, by a statement in writing whether the merger is approved, subject to conditions or prohibited. The court is required to sanction the scheme of arrangement.

[345] Upon approval by the Commission and the court order sanctioning the scheme, the applicant is required to file the following:

(a) a copy of the court order sanctioning the scheme within seven days of the court making the order;
(b) a copy of the newspaper publication of the court order;
(c) a statement of the actual cost of the scheme;
(e) a notification of the completion or otherwise of the exercise within three months of the court's order; and
(f) summary reports of the scheme.

15.2 Notification and Implementation of Large Mergers

[346] It is pertinent to note that the FCCPA makes no mention of Intermediate Mergers, however by virtue of the Joint Advisory issued by the FCCPC and SEC, the existing SEC Rules are still applicable to Mergers and Acquisitions. The SEC Rules categorize mergers into three namely; small, intermediate and large mergers.

[347] A party to a large merger shall notify the FCCPC of that merger in the prescribed manner and form.

[348] In the case of a large merger, the primary acquiring company and the primary target company shall each provide a copy of the notice contemplated in section 96(1) of FCCPA to:

(a) any registered trade union that represents the employees in the acquiring and target undertakings respectively; or
(b) the employees or representatives of the employees of the acquiring and target undertakings, if there are no such registered trade unions.

[349] The parties to a large merger shall not implement the merger until it has been approved with or without conditions by the FCCPC.

15.3 Large Merger Procedure Before FCCPC

[350] Within sixty business days after the parties to a large merger have fulfilled all notification requirements referred to in section 96 of the FCCPA, the FCCPC:

(a) may extend the period in which it has to consider the proposed merger to 120 business days and issue an extension notice to all parties to the merger; or
(b) after having considered the merger in accordance with the provisions of this Act, issue a report in the prescribed form:
    (i) approving the merger,

(ii) approving the merger subject to conditions, or
(iii) prohibiting implementation of the merger.

[351] The Commission shall:

(a) give to the parties applying for approval of a large merger its decision and cause a notice of the decision to be published in at least two national newspapers; and
(b) issue written reasons for its decision where:
  (i) it prohibits or conditionally approves the merger, or
  (ii) it is requested to do so by a party to the merger.

[352] A person aggrieved by the Commission's decision under this Part may file an application for review before the Tribunal and where the decision relates to a decision of the Tribunal, to the Court of Appeal.

15.4 Procedure for Obtaining Approval

[353] Because of the high potential of mergers and acquisitions to create monopoly powers and, therefore, jeopardize competition and the development of a free-market economy, SEC in its regulations has outlined three broad steps before its approval can be given for any merger or acquisition. By virtue of the new regulatory regime in mergers and acquisition transactions in Nigeria, the FCCPC is saddled with the responsibility of approving mergers. These steps are still applicable pursuant to the Joint Advisory issued by the FCCPC and SEC. These steps are:

(1) filing a pre-merger notification for evaluation;
(2) filing a formal application for approval of the proposed merger; and
(3) complying with post-approval requirements.

[354] The necessary requirements of the above-outlined steps include the following.

15.5 Pre-merger Notification

[355] A pre-merger notification may be filed by submitting to the Commission a report that must contain the following information and documents:

(1) A copy of the letter appointing the Financial Adviser(s).
(2) Extract of Board Resolutions of the merging companies authorizing the merger duly certified by a Director and the Company Secretary.
(3) Copy of the certificate of incorporation certified by the Company Secretary.

(4) CAC certified true copy of the Particulars of Director (i.e., Form CAC7).
(5) Letter of 'No Objection' from the regulators of the company's industrial sector (where applicable, for specialized industries).
(6) The audited accounts of the merging entities for the preceding five years or the number of years any of the companies have been in operation if less than five years.
(7) Applicable merger notification fee.
(8) Letters of intent signed by the merging companies accompanied by board resolutions supporting the merger.
(9) A detailed description of the proposed transaction, including all the background studies relating to the merger and the justifications for it.
(10) Detailed information about the product lines or operations of the companies.
(11) A list of the major competitors in that product market and the market position or market share of each company.
(12) The structure and organization of the merging companies, etc.
(13) An analysis of the effect of the acquisition on the relevant market, including the post-acquisition market position of the acquiring or surviving company.
(14) The latest financial statement of the companies.

15.6 Formal Application

[356] A formal application seeking the approval of a proposed merger, acquisition or combination must be filed after receipt of a favourable response to the pre-merger notification from the Commission and must be accompanied by the following:

(1) An agreement for a merger/acquisition containing the following, among other things:
- terms and conditions of the merger/acquisition; and
- mode of carrying out the merger/acquisition;

(2) Resolutions adopted by the shareholders of each company involved in the merger/acquisition approving the merger/acquisition agreement.
(3) A comprehensive joint write-up by the issuing Houses in respect of the proposals in the merger package indicating business lines and stating reasons for the merger – that is, the synergy effects, etc.
(4) Five years audited Accounts of all the enterprises involved (including detailed Profit and Loss Accounts) if the fusion would involve the exchange of shares. However, if it would involve sale for cash, then only the accounts of the enterprise(s), being taken over, would be required.
(5) Draft Scheme of Arrangement (if any).
(6) A statement that the Certificate of Incorporation of one of the constituted companies shall be the certificate of the surviving or resultant company (where applicable).

(7) The mode of converting the shares of each constituent company into shares or other securities of the surviving or resultant company and, if there are no exchange of shares or securities, the cash, property, rights or securities of any other company that the shareholders of the constituent companies are to receive in exchange for, or upon conversion of such shares and the surrender of their share certificates; which cash, property rights or securities of another company may be in addition to or in lieu of shares or other securities of the surviving or resulting company.

(8) The signatures of the Chairman of the Board of Directors or the Chief Executive and attested to by the Secretary of each of the constituent companies on prescribed application documents.

[357] While attention would be focused on these minimum procedural requirements, different applications may be characterized by different peculiarities. It should, however, be noted that a merger case involving the exchange of shares between two or more companies cannot be handled by an Issuing House singularly. Each company involved in the merger has to be represented by an Issuing House.

15.7 Post-approval Requirements

[358] The post-approval requirements include the following:

(1) the submission of the court's order sanctioning the Scheme of Arrangement; and

(2) notification of the completion of the merger exercise.

15.8 Party Responsible for Filing Application

[359] Generally, the acquiring company files for the approval if a merger or acquisition is proposed. In the case of a merger or combination resulting in a new company, any of the constituent companies may file the application. Filing may be done through an authorized professional agent (Issuing House registered by the SEC) on behalf of the company.

[360] A merger/acquisition shall not be deemed as consummated until after approval of the FCCPC is obtained. During the period of review, preliminary negotiations and steps may be pursued by the companies. The FCCPC may, during this period, based on information available from the application, decide to investigate further the proposed transaction instead of reviewing only the documents filed before it.

15.9 Power to Acquire Shares of Dissenting Shareholder

[361] Where a scheme or contract (not being a takeover bid under Part XII of ISA involving the transfer of shares or any class of shares in a company (in this section referred to as *the transferor company*) to another company, whether a company within the meaning of ISA or not (in this section referred to as *the transferee company*) has, within four months after the making of the offer in that behalf by the transferee company, been approved by the holders of not less than nine-tenths in value of the shares whose transfer is involved (other than shares already held at the date of the offer by, or by a nominee for the transferee company or its subsidiary), the transferee company may at any given time within two months after the expiration of the said four months give notice in the prescribed manner to any dissenting shareholder that it desires to acquire his shares.

[362] When a notice under section 129(1) of ISA is given, the transferee company shall be entitled and bound to acquire those shares on the terms on which, under the scheme or contract, the shares of the approving shareholders are to be transferred to the transferee company unless on an application made by the dissenting shareholder within one month from the date on which the notice was given the court thinks it fit to order otherwise.

[363] Where shares in the transferor company of the said class or classes as the shares whose transfer is involved are already held as specified in section 129(1) of this section to a value greater than one-tenth of the aggregate of their value and that of the share (other than already held as specified in the said subsection) whose transfer is involved, the foregoing provisions of this section shall not apply unless:

(a) the transferee company offers the same terms to all holders of the shares (other than those already held as aforesaid) whose transfer is involved, or where those shares include shares, of different classes, of each class of them; and
(b) the holders who approve the scheme or contract besides holding not less than nine-tenths in value of the shares (other than those already held as aforesaid) whose transfer is involved shall not be less than three-quarters in number of the holders of those shares.

[364] Where a notice has been given by the transferee company under section 129(1) of ISA and the court has not, on an application made by the dissenting shareholder, ordered to the contrary, the transferee company shall:

(a) on the expiration of one month from the date on which the notice has been given, or if an application has been disposed of, transmit a copy of the notice to the transferor company together with an instrument of transfer executed on behalf of the shareholder by any person appointed by the transferee company and on its behalf by the transferee company;
(b) pay or transfer to the transferor company the amount or other consideration representing the price payable by the transferee company for the shares which by virtue of this section the company is entitled to acquire, and the

transferor company shall thereupon register the transferee company as the holder of those shares.

[365] Any sums received by the transferor company under this section shall be paid into a separate bank account, and any such sums and any other consideration so received shall be held by that company on trust for the several persons entitled to the shares in respect of which said sums or other consideration were respectively received.

[366] In this section, 'dissenting shareholder' includes a shareholder who has not assented to the scheme or contract and any shareholder who has failed or refused to transfer to the transferee company in accordance with the scheme or contract.

15.10 Right of Dissenting Shareholder to Compel Acquisition of Shares

[367] This section shall apply where, in pursuance of any such scheme of merger, shares are transferred to another company or its nominee, and those shares together with any other shares in the first-mentioned company held by a nominee for the transferee company or its subsidiary at the date of the transfer comprise or include nine-tenths in value of the shares in the first-mentioned company or of any class of those shares.

[368] The transferee company shall, within one month from the date of the transfer (unless on previous transfer in pursuance of the scheme or contract it has already complied with this requirement), give notice of that fact in the prescribed manner to the holder of the remaining shares or of the remaining shares of that class, as the case may be, who have not assented to the scheme or contract.

[369] Any such holder may, within three months from the giving of the notice require the transferee company to acquire the shares in question.

[370] If a shareholder gives notice under section 129(3) of ISA with respect to any shares, the transferee company shall be entitled and bound to acquire those shares on the terms on which under the scheme or contract the shares of the approving shareholders were transferred to it, or on such other terms as may be agreed on as the court hearing the application of either the transferee company or the shareholder thinks fit.

16 ANTI-MONOPOLY ENFORCEMENT: REVOCATION OF MERGER APPROVAL

[371] By virtue of the FCCPA, the FCCPC regulates M&A and business combinations generally, and the review process is to prevent incidents of monopoly within the market. The Federal Competition and Consumer Protection Act is the extant antitrust/competition law in Nigeria which establishes the Federal Competition

and Consumer Protection Commission and the Competition and Consumer Protection Tribunal for the promotion of competition in the Nigerian markets at all levels by eliminating monopolies, prohibiting abuse of a dominant market position and penalizing other restrictive trade and business practices. The FCCPC is to determine whether or not the merger or proposed merger is likely to substantially prevent or lessen competition, by assessing the factors such as the actual and potential level of import competition in the market, whether the merger or proposed merger will result in the removal of an effective competitor etc.

[372] Section 99(1) of the FCCPA provides that:

> The Commission may revoke its own decision to approve or conditionally approve a small or large merger if:
>
> (a) the decision was based on incorrect information for which a party to the merger is responsible;
> (b) the approval was obtained by deceit;
> (c) the parties fail to implement the merger within 12 months after the approval was granted; or
> (d) an undertaking concerned has breached an obligation attached to the decision of the Commission approving the merger.

16.1 Anti-competition Practices in Regulated Industries

16.1.1 Communications Market

[373] *Exclusive Regulator of Anti-Competition in Communications Market:* The Nigeria Communications Commission (NCC) has exclusive responsibility to determine, pronounce upon, administer, monitor and enforce compliance with competition laws and regulations, as it relates to the Nigerian communications market.

[374] *Anti-Competition Practices:* Licensees are prohibited from engaging in any conduct which has the purpose or effect of substantially lessening competition in any aspect of the Nigerian communications market. The NCC may determine that a licensee is in a dominant position in any aspect of the Nigerian communication market.

[375] The NCC may from time to time publish guidelines or regulations which clarify the meaning of 'substantial lessening of competition' in the Nigeria communications market, and such guidelines or regulations may include references to:

(1) the relevant economic market;
(2) global trends in the relevant market;
(3) the impact of the conduct on the number of competitors in a market and their market shares;
(4) the impact of the conduct on barriers to entry into the market;
(5) the impact of the conduct on the range of services in the market;

(6) the impact of the conduct on the cost and profit structures in the market; and
(7) any other matters which the Commission is satisfied are relevant.

[376] A licensee is prohibited from entering into any understanding, agreement or arrangement, whether legally enforceable or not, which provides for:

(1) rate fixing;
(2) market sharing;
(3) boycott of another competitor;
(4) boycott of a supplier of apparatus or equipment; or
(5) boycott of any other licensee.

[377] A licensee is prohibited at any time or in any circumstance, to make it a condition for the provision or supply of a product or service in a communications market that the person acquiring such product or service in the communications market is also required to acquire or not to acquire any other product or service either from himself or from another person.

[378] *Exemption:* A licensee may apply to the NCC prior to engaging in any conduct which may be construed to have the purpose or effect of substantially lessening competition in any aspect of the Nigerian communications industry, for authorization of the conduct, and the NCC may authorize the conduct if satisfied that the authorization is in the national interest.

16.1.2 Aviation Industry

[379] In the aviation industry, the **Civil Aviation Act, 2006** authorizes the Nigerian Civil Aviation Authority to investigate any case or cases of unfair or deceptive trade practices or methods of competition, including the prices of airline tickets. Where an infringement is found, the Nigerian Civil Aviation Authority is authorized to require the offending party to desist from such antitrust or anti-competition practice.

[380] The FCCPA provides that in so far as the Act applies to an industry or sector of an industry that is subject to the jurisdiction of another government agency by the provisions of any other law, in matters or conducts which affect competition and consumer protection, the FCCPA shall be construed as establishing a concurrent jurisdiction between the Commission and the relevant government agency, with the Commission having precedence over and above the relevant government agency.

[381] The FCCPC shall negotiate agreements with all such government agencies whose mandate includes enforcement of competition and consumer protection for the purpose of coordinating and harmonizing the exercise of jurisdiction over completion and consumer protection matters within the relevant industry or sector, and to ensure the consistent application of the provisions of this Act.

17 TAXATION ASPECTS OF MERGERS AND ACQUISITIONS

17.1 Tax Implication of Mergers and Acquisitions

(Federal Inland Revenue Service (FIRS) Information Circular No. 2006)Statutory Requirement under the Companies Income Tax Act (CITA)

[382] The CITA in section 29(12) Cap. 21 LFN, 2004 provides that

> No merger, take-over, transfer or restructuring of the trade or business carried on by a company shall take place without having obtained the Board's direction under subsection 9 of the section and clearance with respect to any tax that may be due and payable under the Capital Gains Tax Act.

[383] The implication of this provision is that the approval of the Federal Inland Revenue Service is a necessary condition for the completion of the process in a merger or acquisition bid. Therefore, no merger or acquisition bids would be fully consummated without the companies involved having obtained the consent from the FIRS.

Procedure for Obtaining the Board's Approval

[384] From the start, the merging companies are required to submit to the Board, copies of the scheme of merger and scheme of arrangement on the consolidation request for its study and proper evaluation in order to ensure that taxes which may result from the companies' transactions are correctly assessed and collected. Herein lies the relevance of the Board's powers under section 29(9)(c)(i) to require either of the companies directly affected by any direction which is under the consideration of the Board to guarantee or give security to its satisfaction for payment in full of all tax due or to become due by the company which is selling or transferring such asset or business.

Tax Issues in Mergers and Acquisitions

[385] A merger may result in any of the following situations:

(1) Formation of a new company.
(2) Continuation of the consolidated business by one of the merging parties, in its name or under a new name.
(3) Cessation of business by the other merging parties.

[386] In an acquisition, there is only an acquiring company(ies) and the company being acquired.

Emergence of a New Company

Rendition of Annual Returns

[387] Where a new company emerges from a merger process, then, the new company is expected to file its returns, in line with the provisions of section 55(2)(b) of CITA. The section provides that: –

> every new company shall file with the Board, its audited accounts and returns within eighteen months from the date of its incorporation or not later than six months after the end of its first accounting period as defined in section 29(3) of the Act, whichever is earlier.

[388] It should, however, be understood that a mere change of name does not make an existing business entity a new company. Such companies will continue to be treated as old businesses on an ongoing concern basis.

Basis of Assessment

[389] Commencement rule as provided under section 29(3) will apply to the new company, except where any of the under-listed circumstances arise:

(i) where the merging parties are connected parties, the Board may direct that commencement rule be set aside, in which case, the new company will file its returns as an ongoing concern and its assessment will be determined on preceding year basis;
(ii) where the new business is a reconstituted company, taking over the trade or business formerly run by its foreign parent company.

Claim of Allowances

[390] CITA did not categorically address the value, which assets may be transferred for the purpose of capital allowances claim. However, International Financial Reporting Standards 3 (IFRS 3) prescribes that in merger accounting the 'acquisition method' should apply. This generally means that assets acquired and liabilities assumed are to be measured at their fair values at the acquisition date.

Unabsorbed Losses and Un-Utilized Capital Allowances Brought Forward

[391] The new company may also not be permitted to inherit the unabsorbed losses and capital allowances of the absorbed companies, except under the following circumstance:

(i) where a reconstituted company is carrying on the same business previously carried on by this company, and it is proved that the losses have not been allowed against any assessable profits or income of that company for any such year; in that case, the amount of unabsorbed losses shall be deemed to be a loss incurred by the reconstituted company in its trade or business during the year of assessment in which the business commenced.

Taxes and deductibility of Related Expenses

[392]

(i) **Stamp Duties:** Duty payment will arise on the share capital of the new company, subject to the provisions of the Stamp Duties Act, in relation to capital and duty relief.
(ii) **Consolidated Expenses:** Fees paid to statutory bodies such as SEC, NSE, CBN, Land Authorities, etc., including professionals like Accountants, Stockbrokers, Issuing Houses, and Solicitors, are regarded as capital in nature and will, therefore, not be allowed as deductible expenses by virtue of CITA.
(iii) **Taxation of Consolidation Fees**: Fees paid to professionals for services rendered in connection with consolidation will be subject to Value Added Tax (VAT) and Withholding Tax (WHT) at the rates of 7.5% and 10% respectively.

Tax Indemnification

[393] CITA provides that the Board may require the new company to guarantee or give security for payment in full, for any tax due or that may become due by any of the ceased companies.

Status of a Surviving Company in Relation to Taxation

[394] It is a possibility that one of the merging companies survives and retains its old name or a new name to inherit the assets, liabilities, reserves and entire operations of the merging parties. Where this happens, the following points must be noted:

(i) the surviving company must file its returns in line with the provisions of section 55(2)(a) of CITA;
(ii) commencement rules under section 29(3) of CITA will **not** apply to the surviving company, as it will be regarded as an existing company;
(iii) the surviving company will **not** be allowed to claim investment allowance on the assets which were transferred to it and will not claim the initial allowance on assets;
(iv) the surviving company may, however, claim annual allowance only on the Tax Written Down Values (TWDV) of the assets transferred to it;
(v) the surviving company may not inherit the unabsorbed losses and capital allowances of the merging companies, except if it is proved that the new business is a reconstituted company;
(vi) all expenses paid by the surviving company in connection with the merger or consolidation exercise are to be regarded as capital in nature and non-deductible for the purpose of tax;
(vii) all fees payable on merger bids or consolidation will be liable to VAT and WHT just like it is applicable to the emergence of a new company. Stamp duties will be paid on the increase in share capital, and the company will

have to obtain its own staff pension scheme approval from the Joint Tax Board (JTB).

Ceased Businesses

[395] The merger or consolidation exercise may also result in cessation of business for any of the merging parties. In this case, cessation rule as applicable under section 29(4) of CITA will apply to any of the merging companies which have now ceased business permanently, except if any of the following circumstances occur:

(i) where the merging companies are connected. Here, the Board may direct, in line with its discretionary powers, under section 29(9) of CITA that the cessation rule may not apply;
(ii) where a reconstituted company is formed to take over the trade or business formerly run by its foreign parent company (*see* section 29(10) of CITA).

Capital Gains Tax on Assets in Business Re-organizations

[396] Section 32 of Capital Gains Tax Act (CGTA) (as amended by the Finance Act 2019) provides that where a trade or business carried on by a company is sold or transferred to a Nigerian company for the purposes of better organization of that trade or business or the transfer of its management to Nigeria, and any asset employed in such trade or business is sold or transferred, no tax shall apply under this Act to the sale or transfer of the assets to the extent that one company has control over the other or both are controlled by some other person or are members of a recognized group of companies and have been so for a consecutive period of at least 365 days prior to the date of reorganization; provided that if the acquiring company were to make a subsequent disposal of the assets acquired within the succeeding 365 days after the date of transaction, any concession enjoyed under this subsection shall be rescinded and the companies shall be treated as if they did not qualify for the concession stipulated in this subsection as at the date of initial reorganization.

Effect of Taxation on Consolidation for Acquiring/Acquired Companies

[397] The tax implications of consolidation on acquiring company or acquired companies are similar to those of mergers. Acquisition expenses are non-deductible while fees paid to professional bodies are equally liable to WHT and VAT.

Clarifications

[398] The Federal Board of Inland Revenue has made the clarification contained in this circular for the benefit of companies which may be considering merger options. The FIRS has no power under the Act to halt or prevent any merger proposals, once the steps are in line with the requirements of CAMA. The Board's concern, however, lies with ensuring that all taxes due or may be payable by any of the merging companies are assessed and fully recovered. For this reason, companies intending to merge or consolidate, are advised to promptly bring such a proposal to the notice of the FIRS with copies of relevant schemes of Merger and Arrangement for evaluation. The benefit for the taxpayer is that the acquiring company enjoys the privilege of not having to pay taxes that could have arisen from the computation of taxes on the company that was acquired on cessation.

18 EMPLOYMENT CONSIDERATION

[399] In the process of evaluating any proposed merger/acquisition scheme, the FCCPC places great emphasis on the likely impact that such a scheme, if approved, would have on employees of the affected company or companies. The regulatory expectation is that no scheme would be approved if it would have the effect of placing the employees on terms that are less beneficial than their present contracts of employment.

[400] The FCCPA requires that the primary acquiring undertaking and the primary target undertaking in a large merger shall each provide a copy of the notification furnished to the FCCPC to:

(a) any registered trade union that represents the employees in the acquiring and target undertakings respectively; or
(b) the employees or representatives of the employees of the acquiring and target undertakings, if there are no such registered trade unions.

[401] Also, when determining whether a merger or proposed merger can or cannot be justified on the grounds of public interest, the FCCPC shall consider the effect that the merger or proposed merger will have on employment.

[402] Section 134(6) ISA also specifically prescribes that:

> For the purpose of deciding whether or not to grant an 'authority to proceed' with a takeover bid, the SEC shall have regard only to the likely effect of the takeover bid if successfully made:
>
> (a) on the economy of Nigeria;
> (b) on any policy of the Federal Government with respect to manpower and development; and
>
> If satisfied that none of the matters referred to in (a) and (b) above would be adversely affected, SEC would grant an 'authority to proceed' with the proposed takeover bid, but if not so satisfied, it shall refuse to do so.

[403] The Labour Act also provides that the transfer of any contract from one employer to another shall be subject to the consent of the worker and the endorsement of the transfer upon the contract by an authorized labour officer.

19 ACCOUNTING TREATMENT

[404] All financial institutions and public companies in Nigeria are required to have adopted the International Financial Reporting Standards (IFRS) by 2013.

[405] A number of accounting and valuation issues must be satisfactorily addressed in all M&A transactions in Nigeria. SEC demands that each party to the transaction should engage independent financial advisers.

19.1 Consideration

[406] If for instance, it is agreed to merge Company B with Company A, by a process whereby the shareholders of Company B are obliged to surrender their shares in return for shares in Company A, the valuation of the two sets of shares in question becomes a major accounting issue.

19.2 Reporting Accountants Report

[407] All companies in Nigeria must prepare and file audited financial statements annually. For purposes of M&A transactions, these financial statements are reviewed and certified by independent accounting firms who must confirm that these statements give a true and fair view of the state of affairs of the company and of its profits and application of funds for each of the relevant years in question. In addition, a reporting accountant is expected to review the profits forecast prepared by the directors and to confirm the veracity or otherwise of the same.

APPENDIX A: CONFIDENTIALITY AND NON-DISCLOSURE AGREEMENT

THIS CONFIDENTIALITY AND NON-DISCLOSURE AGREEMENT is made this .... day of ....20......

By and Between

EUREKA RESOURCES PLC, a Company incorporated under the laws of Nigeria with registration no. RC . . . ., and having its registered address at . . . . (hereinafter referred to as '**DISCLOSER**'),

And

*[*Name, Status of Establishment and Address of Other Party/Parties] (hereinafter referred to as* '**RECIPIENT**').

Hereinafter, each of the above is individually referred to as a 'Party' and collectively as 'the Parties'.

WHEREAS:

A) The RECIPIENT is interested in entering into discussions with DISCLOSER concerning a possible investment or business combination or arrangement between the Parties (the Business Purpose).
B) In order to evaluate the prospects and advisability of the Business Purpose, RECIPIENT believes it needs to receive and analyse certain confidential and proprietary information of DISCLOSER including, legal, technical, financial, regulatory, operational and other information concerning the DISCLOSER and its business.
C) DISCLOSER is willing to make such information available to RECIPIENT on a confidential basis, only for the purpose of analysis in connection with the Business Purpose and subject to the confidentiality and non-disclosure provisions, terms and conditions set forth in this Agreement.

NOW THEREFORE, in consideration of the mutual covenants and agreements contained herein, Discloser and Recipient agree as follows:

1. CONFIDENTIAL INFORMATION

The RECIPIENT acknowledges and agrees that all information made available by DISCLOSER to RECIPIENT in connection with the Business Purpose regardless of the manner in which it has been furnished, including, without limitation, any and all financial information, technical data, customer lists, sales, marketing and business plans, operating procedures, personnel data and agreements, whether or not such information is oral and if orally disclosed, subsequently confirmed as confidential in writing, written, printed, contained on computer disc or otherwise represented, is the confidential and proprietary information of DISCLOSER (the Confidential Information). The term Confidential Information as used herein also includes: (a) the fact that the Parties may be or are engaged in discussions regarding the Business Purpose and any proposed terms or conditions of or relating to the proposed Business Purpose (b) any and all analyses, compilations, studies or other documents or records prepared by RECIPIENT or any of RECIPIENT's employees, representatives, agents or advisors that contain or otherwise reflect or are generated from Confidential Information.

2. NON-DISCLOSURE OR NON-USE

The RECIPIENT shall hold in strict confidence the Confidential Information, and the RECIPIENT shall not, directly or indirectly: (a) use or permit the use of any of the Confidential Information for, or in connection with, any business of the RECIPIENT, or by any other person whatsoever, or for any purpose other than the analysis of the Business Purpose contemplated hereby, or (b) disclose or permit the disclosure of any of the Confidential Information to any person or entity other than the RECIPIENT's employees, representatives or agents, including without limitation, its financial, legal or other professional advisors, whose knowledge of the proposed Business Purpose and access to the Confidential Information is required to perform their duties in connection with the analysis of the proposed Business Purpose and who agree to comply with the confidentiality, non-disclosure and non-use provisions of this Agreement.

3. DISCLOSURE, APPLICATION AND USE OF CONFIDENTIAL INFORMATION

3.1. RECIPIENT shall use the Confidential Information only for the purpose of evaluating the possibility of a business combination or arrangement with DIS-CLOSER.
3.2. RECIPIENT shall hold the Confidential Information in confidence and shall disclose the Confidential Information only to its employees, agents and advisors who have a need to know to evaluate and accomplish the Business Purpose, and who have agreed in writing to be bound by the terms and conditions of this Agreement.
3.3. Recipient will not utilize, employ, exploit or in any other manner whatsoever use the Confidential Information other than for the Business Purpose without the prior written consent of DISCLOSER.

4. UNAUTHORIZED DISCLOSURE

If RECIPIENT becomes aware of any unauthorized disclosure, loss or misuse of the Confidential Information, RECIPIENT shall promptly notify DISCLOSER.

5. STANDARD OF CARE/COMPLIANCE

5.1. RECIPIENT agrees to use at least the same degree of care to protect the Confidential Information as RECIPIENT uses to protect its own confidential information; provided that, without in any way limiting any other obligation or liability of RECIPIENT under this Agreement, RECIPIENT shall take all appropriate action to prevent the unauthorized use or disclosure of the proposed Business Purpose and the Confidential Information and shall take all reasonable precautions to protect and maintain the confidentiality of the Confidential Information.

5.2. The Confidential Information must be stored and handled in such a way as to prevent unauthorised disclosure.

5.3. Confidential Information delivered orally by DISCLOSER shall be put in writing and transmitted by the DISCLOSER to RECIPIENT within fourteen (14) days of its oral delivery. Delivery shall be in accordance with the notice provisions of this Agreement.

6. RETURN OF CONFIDENTIAL INFORMATION

The DISCLOSER may give notice in writing at any time requiring that any part of the Confidential Information disclosed pursuant to this Confidentiality Agreement and any copies thereof be either returned or destroyed, such return or destruction to be combined with a notice to the DISCLOSER to the effect that upon such return or destruction the RECIPIENT has not knowingly retained in its possession or under its control, either directly or indirectly, any Confidential Information or copies thereof, and the RECIPIENT must comply with any such request within fourteen (14) days of receipt of such request, except to the extent the RECIPIENT is advised by its legal counsel that complying with such notice would be prohibited by law. In case of the latter, the RECIPIENT will, in writing, identify the subject Confidential Information and notify the DISCLOSER of the legal reason for non-compliance.

7. INFORMATION NOT DEEMED CONFIDENTIAL/EXCLUDED INFORMATION

This Agreement shall not apply to any portion of the Confidential Information: (a) the RECIPIENT derived from information in the public domain or without assistance of or reference to anything disclosed through the Confidential Information; or (b) becomes a part of the public domain through no fault of the RECIPIENT; or (c) the RECIPIENT acquires outside of the relationship between the parties to this Agreement, from a third party that is lawfully in possession of such Confidential Information and under no obligation of confidence to DISCLOSER; or (d) was lawfully in the RECIPIENT possession before receipt; or (e) is, at any time, developed by employees of the RECIPIENT independently from the Confidential Information; and RECIPIENT can so prove.

8. PERSONS INCLUDED IN DEFINITION OF 'RECIPIENT'

The term 'RECIPIENT' as used herein shall be deemed to include the RECIPIENT and any and all of its affiliates, officers, directors, owners, employees, representatives or agents, including, without limitation, its financial, legal or other professional advisors.

9. COMPLIANCE WITH LEGAL OBLIGATIONS

In the event that RECIPIENT becomes legally compelled (such as by order of court, administrative agency or other governmental body) to disclose Confidential Information, it shall provide DISCLOSER with prompt written notice of such order or obligation, and to the extent possible, an opportunity to seek a protective order or other appropriate means to preserve the confidentiality of the Confidential Information. In the event no such order is issued or no such challenge is undertaken or such challenge is unsuccessful, only that portion of the Confidential Information that is legally required to be disclosed shall be disclosed. The RECIPIENT agrees that any such disclosure shall not cause any of the Confidential Information that was not required to be disclosed to fall within any exception set forth in Clause 7 above.

10. NO COMMITMENT

Nothing in this Agreement imposes on either Party an obligation to enter into any agreement or transaction and in particular will not oblige either Party to enter into any agreement pursuant to the Business Purpose.

11. NO WARRANTIES; ACCESS TO CONFIDENTIAL INFORMATION

The RECIPIENT understands and acknowledges that any and all information contained in the Confidential Information is being provided without any representation or warranty, express or implied, as to the accuracy or completeness of the Confidential Information, on the part of DISCLOSER. The RECIPIENT agrees that neither DISCLOSER nor any of its representatives shall have any liability to RECIPIENT resulting from use of the Confidential Information. The scope of any representations or warranties to be given by DISCLOSER will be negotiated, if at all, along with other terms and conditions in arriving at any mutually acceptable definitive agreement between the parties relating to the transaction, should discussions between the parties progress to such a point. The RECIPIENT acknowledges that DISCLOSER is under no obligation to provide the RECIPIENT with any information, including, without limitation, the Confidential Information, or to give the RECIPIENT access to any portion of DISCLOSER's premises or its employees.

12. NO SOLICITATION

Until the earlier of (a) the execution by the RECIPIENT of a definitive agreement regarding the Business Purpose or (b) three years from the date of this Agreement, the RECIPIENT agrees not to initiate or maintain contact (except for those contacts made in the ordinary course of business) with any officer, director or employee of DISCLOSER regarding the Business Purpose, except with the prior written consent of DISCLOSER. The RECIPIENT agrees not to solicit for employment any of the current employees of DISCLOSER so long as they are empowered by DISCLOSER until the earlier of (a) or (b) described in this Article, without the prior written consent of DISCLOSER.

13. INJUNCTIVE RELIEF

It is understood and agreed that money damages would not be a sufficient remedy for any breach of this Agreement and that DISCLOSER shall be entitled to specific performance and injunctive or other equitable relief as a remedy for any such breach. The RECIPIENT further agrees to waive any requirement for the security or posing of any bond in connection with such remedy. Such remedy shall not be deemed to be the exclusive remedy for a breach of this Agreement, but shall be in addition to all other remedies available at law or equity to DISCLOSER.

14. AMENDMENTS AND ASSIGNMENT

No amendment to or assignment of the benefit of any of the provisions of this Agreement will be effective unless consented to in writing by the Parties to this Agreement.

15. NO WAIVER

The failure to enforce or to require the performance at any time of any of the provisions of this Agreement will not be construed to be a waiver of such provision, and will not affect either the validity of this Agreement or any part hereof or the right of any Party thereafter to enforce each and every provision in accordance with the terms of this Agreement.

16. ENTIRE AGREEMENT

This Agreement contains the entire agreement of the Parties with respect to the subject matter of this Agreement and supersedes all prior agreements between or among the Parties, whether written or oral, with respect to the subject matter of this Agreement.

17. AMENDMENTS

Any amendment to this Agreement must be executed in writing by both parties.

18. NOTICES

18.1. All notices, demands or other communications under this Agreement must be given or made in writing, and must be sent by private courier or facsimile, and shall be deemed to be given three (3) days after delivery to the private courier or on transmittal of the facsimile, as follows:-

To DISCLOSER: ______________________________

NAME: ______________________________

ADDRESS: ______________________________

TELEPHONE NO: ______________________________

FAX: ______________________________

E-MAIL: ______________________________

To RECIPIENT: ______________________________

NAME: ______________________________

ADDRESS: ______________________________

TELEPHONE NO: ______________________________

FAX: ______________________________

E-MAIL: ______________________________

Or at such other address or to such fax number as may be designated by notice from such Party.

19. NO TRANSFER OF TITLE, NO LICENCES

19.1. All Confidential Information is acknowledged by the Recipient to be the property of the Discloser and the disclosure of the Confidential Information does not confer any rights to that Confidential Information on the Recipient.

19.2. No license to Recipient is granted or implied by disclosing Confidential Information to that Party.

20. DURATION AND TERMINATION

This Agreement shall take effect on the date hereof and shall continue for one (1) year unless terminated earlier by either party giving thirty (30) days prior written notice to the other party. The Recipient's obligations under this Agreement shall remain in full force and effect for a period of three (3) years after the date of termination.

21. GOVERNING LAW

21.1. This agreement is governed by and will be construed in accordance with the laws of the Federal Republic of Nigeria.

21.2. The Parties submit to the exclusive jurisdiction of the courts of the Federal Republic of Nigeria in relation to any legal actions or proceedings arising out of or in connection with this agreement.

21.3. Process by which any proceedings are begun in Nigeria may be served on any Party by being delivered to the address herein of that Party.

21.4. Damages would not be an adequate remedy for any breach of this Agreement and the Parties shall be entitled to resort to such equitable remedies as are permit-ted under the laws of Nigeria for any threatened or actual breach of this Agreement and no proof of special damages shall be necessary for the enforcement of this Agreement.

22. ARBITRATION

Any dispute under this Agreement shall be settled first by a meeting in person of at least one senior executive officer of each Party. If the latter does not resolve a dispute within fifteen (15) days of the notifying Party's calling of the meeting, either Party may refer the matter to binding arbitration. Arbitration shall be conducted under the rules of UNCITRAL, in Nigeria unless the Parties mutually agree upon another venue. A panel of three (3) arbitrators shall conduct the arbitration; one each appointed by each party and the third appointed by the other two. The arbitrators appointed shall be Nigerians. The Arbitral award shall be binding on the Parties and no right of appeal shall lie. The Parties agree to the Jurisdiction of the appropriate courts in Nigeria and/or the site of the arbitration for the purpose of interim measures and to the jurisdiction of any court of competent jurisdiction for enforcement of the award. The Parties shall share evenly the cost of the arbitration except for their own respective individual costs, which they shall bear individually.

23. AUTHORITY TO EXECUTE

The Parties represent that each has the legal authority to execute this Agreement on behalf of the Person for whom it is signed, and that such signature does in fact bind the Person it purports to so bind.

24. COUNTERPARTS

This Agreement may be executed in six (6) counterparts and any counterpart shall come into force as against any party immediately upon the execution of such counterpart by that Party.

IN WITNESS WHEREOF the parties hereto have affixed their seals and set their hands by their authorized representatives the day and the year first above written.

THE COMMON SEAL OF THE WITHIN-NAMED
EUREKA RESOURCES PLC
WAS AFFIXED IN THE PRESENCE OF

____________________ ____________________

DIRECTOR SECRETARY
THE COMMON SEAL OF THE WITHIN-NAMED
[*Name of **RECIPIENT**]
WAS AFFIXED IN THE PRESENCE OF

____________________ ____________________

DIRECTOR SECRETARY

APPENDIX B: MEMORANDUM OF UNDERSTANDING

BETWEEN

EUREKA RESOURCES PLC

AND

*[*Name of Other Party]*

THIS MEMORANDUM OF UNDERSTANDING is made the.........day of . . . . 20. . . . . .

By and Between

EUREKA RESOURCES PLC, a Company incorporated under the laws of Nigeria with registration no. RC . . . ., and having its registered address at............. (hereinafter referred to as 'ERP')

And

*[*Name, Status of Establishment and Address of Other Party/Parties]*

Hereinafter, each of the above is individually referred to as 'Party' and collectively as 'the Parties'.

WHEREAS:

A. The Parties are desirous of exploring the prospects of an investment and/or business combination or arrangement for the future operations of their respective businesses;
B. **ERP** has constituted a select Committee, as its authorized representatives, to enter into discussions, consider and invite proposals for implementing the businesses combination or arrangement;
C. The other party has constituted a select Committee, as its authorized representatives, to enter into discussions, consider and invite proposals for implementing the business combination or arrangement;
D. The authorized representatives of the Parties shall be engaging in discussions and exchange of information towards the prospects of an investment and/or business combination arrangement;
E. The purpose of the MEMORANDUM OF UNDERSTANDING (MOU) is to summarize the understandings and expectations of each Party and set forth the manner to proceed. The general basis and conditions hereinafter set out in this **MOU** are subject to a formal and final business combination agreement, if any;

F. It is expressly understood that the Parties intend to be legally bound only ifand when a mutually satisfactory business combination agreement covering all of the terms of the transaction is executed and delivered.

In connection with these premises and pursuant to a Confidentiality and Non-Disclosure Agreement executed on the . . . . day of . . . . 20. . . . ., and the mutual covenants set forth herein;

IT IS HEREBY AGREED as follows:

1. EXCLUSIVITY PERIOD

The Parties, through their respective Committee of authorized representatives shall be discussing on the terms and conditions of an investment and/or business combination or arrangement and have not reached an agreement-in-principle. However, in order to proceed with negotiations, the Parties mutually agree that from the . . . . day of 20. . . . . until a period expiring . . . . days thereafter, (the Exclusivity Period) none of the Parties shall directly or indirectly solicit or initiate parallel discussions concerning similar scope of proposals for a business combination or arrangement.

2. HEADS OF AGREEMENT

During the 'Exclusivity Period' the Parties shall continue discussions and negotiations towards a formal business combination agreement predicated on the underlisted Items/Heads of Agreement and other items as may be subsequently identified to be included, viz:

(i) *Business Purpose*
- Scope and Strategic Rationale;
- Shares/Assets to be bought or sold or consolidated;
- Specify excluded items (assets or liabilities);
- Freedom from encumbrances;
- Responsibilities of each Party;

(ii) *Coordinating Committee – (Comprising Duly Authorised Representatives of Each Party)*
- Composition of Coordinating Committee

(iii) *Consideration*
- Price or range of possible values, or price basis; – Form, for example, cash, shares, loan notes, etc.
- Timing of payment (including any retention fund); (iv) *Time Table*
- Exchange of Contracts; – Completion;
- Arrangements between exchange and completion;

(v) *Conditions Precedent*
- Due Diligence;
- Board Approvals;
- Shareholders' Approvals;
- Regulatory Consents, for example, NAICOM, SEC, CAC, Nigerian Stock Exchange

- Tax Clearances;
- Court-sanctioned approvals;
- Specific contracts or consents, for example, Creditor consents; Lessor consents; Insurance;

(vi) *Warranties and Indemnities*
- General Approach to be adopted. (vii) *Restrictive Covenants*
- Non-Competition;
- Non-Solicitation;
- Confidentiality.

(viii) *Employee Matters and Pensions*
- Service contracts with key executives;
- Basis of calculating transfer value for pensions; – Continuity of employment.

(ix) *Exclusivity of Negotiation*
- Time, period involved;
- Accommodation/Joinder of Other Parties.

(x) *Confidentiality*

(xi) *Costs*
- If one party is to bear or indemnify part of the other party's costs, should the transaction be abandoned?

(xii) *Transactional Documents and Agreements to be Negotiated*
- Exclusivity and Break Fee Agreement;
- Disclosure Letter;
- Business Combination Agreement;
- Scheme of Merger/Business Combination

IN WITNESS WHEREOF, the Parties hereto have caused their duly authorized representatives to append their signatures and common seals hereto the day and year first above written.

THE COMMON SEAL of the within-named

EUREKA RESOURCES PLC

was hereto affixed in the presence of:

____________________ ____________________

DIRECTOR SECRETARY

THE COMMON SEAL of the within-named

*[*Other Party/Parties]*

was hereto affixed in the presence of:

____________________ ____________________

DIRECTOR SECRETARY

APPENDIX C: LEGAL DUE DILIGENCE

CHECKLIST OF DOCUMENTS

- Please provide all relevant documents in relation to the items indicated in this Checklist of Documents including all schedules, appendices and attachments. If a document, license, permit or approval provided to us has been amended, suspended, terminated or cancelled or there is any reason to believe that this will happen, please provide full details.
- Where a request is not applicable please mark the question N/A and please explain why.
- If the Company has any sub-entity with independent legal person status, the sub-entity should be regarded as another 'Company' and should separately provide answers and all relevant documents in relation to the items indicated in this Checklist of Documents.
- If prior to the completion of the proposed transaction there is any change in relation to any answer and/or document provided hereunder, please update us immediately.

S/N	DOCUMENT	AVAILABLE	NON AVAILABLE	COMMENTS
1.	**THE CONSTITUTION DOCUMENTS OF THE TARGET COMPANY** • Certificate of Incorporation. • Memorandum & Articles of Association. • Statement of Authorized Share Capital FORMCAC 2. • Particulars of Directors Form CAC 7. • Particulars of Registered Address Form CAC 3. • Annual Returns & Financial Statement for the last 3 years together with copies of filing receipts in respect thereof. • Certificate of change of name. • Details of any subsidiaries of the Company, including name, country of incorporation/registration, place of business, nature of business and the extent of the Company's share-holding therein. • Certificate of Registration of any trade or business name used by the Company other than the name of the Company. • Organizational chart and description of the Company's organizational structure. • Any other relevant constitutive documents, together with any amendments, and evidence of due and valid registration with the related governing authorities.			

2	**CORPORATE INFORMATION OWNERSHIP** • Particulars of Shareholders Form CAC 2. • Beneficial Ownership Structure of corporate shareholders & affiliated companies. • Background information of the shareholders of the Company. • A certified copy of the Register of Members. • Documents evidencing full details of dividends paid or declared by the Company in the last five years. • Documents evidencing any increase in authorized and/or share capital of the Company from incorporation to date. There would include the relevant special resolutions, statement of increase of nominal capital, notice of increase of share capital together with the relevant filing receipts at the companies registry in relation to change in share capital. • All documents relating to any restructuring process including but not limited to transfer of assets, business, employees and any other transactions carried out during the restructuring process. • Details of any subsidiaries of the Company and description on establishment of any subsidiary, branch, operational office, distribution center, representative office or any other business operated or investment (such as joint ventures or stocks or equity investments) made by the Company. **Board And Management Of The Company** • Particulars of the directors and copies of the resolutions or other document appointing each of them to the office of director. • Copies of the service contracts of the managing director, and all other executive directors.

S/N	DOCUMENT	AVAILABLE	NON AVAILABLE	COMMENTS
	• Copies of any agreements for the provision of management, technical or other similar services to which the Company is a party. • A summary of the terms of any outstanding loans granted to or by the Company to any of its directors and or any guarantees provided by the Company to such directors. • All existing powers of attorney granted by the Company.			
	Company Documents • Minutes of meetings of the Board of Directors held during the 3 most recent fiscal years. • Resolutions and Minutes of shareholders' meetings held during the 3 most recent fiscal years. • Copies of resolutions effecting and notification of change in name or registered address of the Company. • Auditor's reports and details of the Company's auditors and professional advisors for the last 3 years.			
3	**MATERIAL CONTRACTS & AGREEMENTS** • All Shareholders Agreements, investment agreements, promoter's agreements and agreements for establishing the Company and any other arrangements or letters of entered into between any shareholder or any its affiliates and the Company relating to any matter or equity of the Company relating to any matter or equity of the Company or which would grant to any third party any right that would have damage or affect the right of the shareholders. • Memorandum of Understanding/ Investors Agreement.			

- Any share subscription agreements, partnership/Joint Venture Agreement, shareholder loan agreements or other relevant agreements regulating the relationship of shareholders with the company, and the shareholders.
- All contracts or documents regarding loan or debt of the Company.
- Financial agreements or arrangement, for instance, shareholder loans, lending and finance lease between enterprises.
- Any contract not entered into in the ordinary course of the Company's business or on arm's length terms.
- Any other contract which involves any party which is, or is connected with, one of the affiliates or shareholders of the Company or any current or former director or employee of the Company or their families.
- Contracts, agreements or other legal documents requiring, inhibiting or restricting the Company to add registered capital, transfer stock equity, or adopt any other means to dispose of registered capital or stock equity.
- All other legal documents including without limitation the following:
  - Royalties/Licensing/Franchise Agreement(s)
- Software Agreements
- Consulting Agreements
- Technology Transfer Agreements
- Service Agreements/Third Party Contracts
- Trade Union Agreements
- Guarantees, Indemnities or Financial Arrangement Contracts
- Supply, Sales, Distribution or Service Contract
- Management contracts
- Profit-share Agreements
- Intellectual Property Agreements (trademarks, patents etc.)

S/N	DOCUMENT	AVAILABLE	NON AVAILABLE	COMMENTS
4	**<u>COMPLIANCE - LICENSES, APPROVALS, PERMITS AND CONSENTS</u>** • Copies of all registrations, approvals, licenses, consents, permits and exemptions at any time required with respect to the business carried on by the Company and confirmation that all fees due in relation to such consents have been paid and any conditions thereof, complied with. In particular provide copies of the following: • License or Certificate of Telecom frequency & spectrum and numbering resources • Governmental & Regulatory Permits/Approvals/licenses e.g. NCC, NOTAP, CBN, SON, State, and Municipal authorities e.t.c. • Expatriate Quotas • Tax Clearance Certificates • VAT License • Certificate(s) of Capital Importation • The Company's status of fulfillment of all the requirements for applying and maintaining the said licenses and permits. • Details with regard to any threat to remove any consent or license, attach a new condition to any consent or suspend any consent by any of the relevant respective parties. • Details of any allegations made against the Company by any governmental, administrative or other public authority for non-compliance with any statutory obligations which would or may result in the revocation or withdrawal of any license or consent relevant to the business of the Company (excluding any environmental matters); and details or any threat of revocation of withdrawal of any license or consent relevant to the business of the Company.			

5 **INDEBTEDNESS**

- Loan Agreements
- Mortgage and/or Debenture Security Agreements
- Other borrowing/financing documents (e.g. trade financing or receivable financing documents)
- Copies of (or where not in writing, details of) any agreements or documents relating to any loans, mortgage, pledge, guarantee, other forms of security or letters of comfort made or given by the Company to or in favor of any party.

6 **TITLES TO ASSETS (PREMISES, MOVABLE AND NON-MOVABLE ASSETS)**

- Title Documents over movable & non-movable Assets (Tenancies, Ownership of Premises, Hire Purchase, Equipment Leases, etc.) for or against the Company including without limitation the following:
  - Details of all property owned, leased, occupied or used by the Company including copies of title deeds, leases or licenses held by the Company and its subsidiaries and all relevant information including without limitation the user, address, area, value, title, status, mortgage, annual rent and lease term, tenure, area and site plans.
- Description of all lease agreements with the Company as a lessor or lessee in respect of real property and other fixed assets.
- Details of any encumbrances over any of the material assets and in particular description of all mortgage contracts, assets evaluation reports and mortgage registration documents with authorities.
- Company's register of assets, including description of all assets of the Company and any assets evaluation and appraisal
- A copy of the latest valuation of all assets and a general description of the condition of the key assets.

S/N	DOCUMENT	AVAILABLE	NON AVAILABLE	COMMENTS
	• A copy of the latest valuation of all assets and a general description of the condition of the key assets. • Copies of any maintenance agreements or other contracts relating to the material assets. • Full particulars of any new equipment ordered by the Company but not yet delivered or not yet invoiced including the value and the intended use of this equipment.			
7	**HUMAN RESOURCES / PERSONNEL MATTERS** • A list of all current employees of the Company indicating their name, age, sex, nationality, department, position, annual base salary, primary place of work, whether they are full-time or part-time, years of service, whether they are employed under fixed term or open contracts and whether they have entered into written employment contracts with the Company. • Details of any debtor-creditor relationship between the Company and its employees and how it to be resolved. • Details of the key personnel and succession plans. • Copies of standard employment contracts with employees. • Copies of terms of employment for all senior managers/ standard employment contract with management. • Details of any trade union recognition and copies of any collective labour agreements. Please also provide a copy of any collective bargaining agreement to which the Company is a party. • Details of any employee benefit schemes (including long service, severance and scholarship schemes including expiration dates where applicable). • Incentive scheme of the Company (such as commission, bonus, stock option plan and stock incentive plan) and the method for determining such scheme			

- Description of all benefit and retirement schemes for employees, including but not limited to profit sharing and bonus scheme, pension scheme, remuneration package, holidays.
- Any related documents including without limitation:
  - HR Conditions of Service
- Schedule of Employees – Managerial & Non-Managerial
- Employee & Directors Contracts, including any Employee Share Ownership Scheme;
- Standard or model Employment letter for workers, employees and executives
- Standard Dismissal letter
- Pension Schemes
- Employee Health Plan Contracts

8 **<u>INSURANCES</u>**

- Insurance Policies held in the past 3 years, such as property insurance, automobile insurance, physical damage insurance or other insurance, and evidence of payment of premium with, in respect of each policy, details of, renewal dates, annual premiums, amount of cover, risk covered, name of relevant insurance company, and policy number.
- Any documentation relating to claims which have been made under such policies in the past three years or circumstances which might give rise to a claim being made

9 **<u>CLAIMS AND LITIGATION</u>**

- Particulars of Pending claims and litigation, mediation or arbitration or any other disputes with third parties in which the Company is involved, which may lead to litigation, arbitration, mediation or other dispute resolution procedures, including the details of the Advocates representing the Company in each matter.
- Court Judgments, declarations or orders for or against the Company.

S/N	DOCUMENT	AVAILABLE	NON AVAILABLE	COMMENTS
	• Copies of any notices received by the Company from any government authority relating to allegations of non-compliance with any rules, regulations or laws applicable to the Company. • Details of any current or pending investigation by any competent authority or any notifications or request from any regulatory or governmental agency affecting the Company including government or court report, order, sanction on environmental liabilities. • Details of any disciplinary, investigation or enforcement action or sanction (including fines or penalties) by Regulators in respect of the Company in the last 5 years. • Lawyers letter of Certification to Auditors (on pending and threatened claims) – latest.			
10	**ENVIRONMENTAL, HEALTH AND SAFETY ('EHS')** • EHS Licenses and approvals • Any government or court report, order, injunction, opinion, approval, sanction, correspondence or claims of any third parties in respect of environmental damage or liability • Any commitments, plans or arrangements made by the Company to any competent government authorities in connection with environmental protection issues and the implementation thereto			

11	**INTELLECTUAL PROPERTY** • Details of all trade mark registrations, brands, patents, service marks, copyrights know-how, domain name, etc.; and registered intellectual property rights owned or relied on directly or indirectly by the Company for the purpose of carrying out its business and confirmation that they have been protected at law. In particular, details of the wireless broadband multi-media technology and the documents evidencing the rights thereto owned by the company. Where the Company uses any intellectual property under a license or user agreement, please provide copies thereof. • All agreements relating to registered or unregistered intellectual property right, including but not limited to trademarks, service marks, domain names, logos, patents, designs, copyrights and know-how including (but not limited to) license agreements or assignment of intellectual property right, if any. • Details of any actual or alleged infringements by third parties of any intellectual property rights owned by or licensed to the Company. • Details of any allegations made against the Company that it has done anything which infringes any other person's intellectual property and any circumstances known to the Company which may give rise to such allegation. • All agreements, licenses or arrangements to which the Company is a party affecting the Intellectual Property Rights (IPR) vested in, or used by, the Company (or where such agreements, licenses or arrangements are not in writing a summary of their terms, including the names of the parties, commencement date, termination date and the termination provisions). • Details of any prohibition on assignment of any IPR.

S/N	DOCUMENT	AVAILABLE	NON AVAILABLE	COMMENTS
12	**<u>BUSINESS ARRANGEMENT</u>** • Any standard terms for the supply of materials and/or services to the Company (a copy of each standard terms of supply is required if there are more than one) and copies of all material supply agreements to which the Company is a party. • List of major customers and major suppliers of the Company over last 3 years. Details of loss of any major customer or supplier of the Company in last 3 years. • Any standard terms of business on which the Company carries on business with (a copy of each standard terms of business is required if there are more differences). • Agreements with any customers or suppliers which differ from standard terms of business. • Other agreements or arrangements which have a material impact on the Company's business or operations.			
13	**<u>TAX</u>** • Tax category and rate applied to the Company and statement on payment of tax due. • Details of any tax preferential treatment, tax exemption or rebate accorded to the Company and relevant governmental approvals or other documentary proof. • Correspondence and other documents relating to any ongoing tax audit (if any) by any tax authority. • Details of any penalty imposed on or any claim asserted against the Company by any tax authority in the past three years, and any potential penalty or claim by any tax authority.			

14	**COMPETITION** • Agreements, or if not applicable, short description of any arrangements that may limit the Company's liberty to make individual commercial decisions. • Details together with copies of any agreements or arrangements, decisions by any government agencies or any legal entities, relating to the Company's business (whether written or oral and whether intended to be legally enforceable or not) which have or could have an object or effect of prevention, distortion or restriction of competition. • Copies of any filings with Competition Authorities, whether national or international, copies of any documentation sent to or from any such authority and details of any outstanding notices or communications with such Authority. • Information concerning all carried out or expected investigations of the Competition Authorities and copies of all correspondence in relation thereto. • Details together with copies of any agreement or arrangements with one or more competitors (whether written or unwritten and whether intended to be legally enforceable or not) which relate to prices or conditions of sale under which utilities or services are to be rendered by the Company.
15	**MISCELLANEOUS** • Any other documents, agreements and correspondence not requested elsewhere in this document which contain information which is or may be material to the proposed acquisition by a third party of an interest in the Company (including without limitation any licenses, approvals, agreements or arrangements which may be affected by the proposed acquisition, such as agreements requiring notice or consent for the proposed acquisition or will become terminable as a result of the acquisition).

APPENDIX C1: FORM OF REPORT ON MATERIAL CONTRACTS

Date of Agreement:	
Parties:	
Brief description of the Agreement:	
Price:	1. What is the charging basis? 2. Any fee cap?
Term:	1. What is the commencement date? 2. What is the termination date?
Termination:	1. What is the notice period for termination? 2. Any compensation payable for termination? 3. Any other early termination provisions?
Confidentiality:	1. Is there any confidentiality provision? 2. Is target Company in breach of this confidentiality provision by disclosing this Agreement?
Limitation/exclusion of liabilities:	1. Did any party exclude or limit its liabilities? 2. Is the limitation or exclusion of liabilities likely to be enforceable?
Warranties, guarantees, indemnities:	Any warranties or indemnities given by one party or another? If so, please state:
Assignment:	1. Is the Agreement assignable? 2. Any consent of third **party** needed for its assignment?

Change of control:	Does a change of control affect the Agreement? If so, please state:
Execution of the Agreement:	1. Has the **AGREEMENT** been properly executed? 2. Did the person **SIGNING** have the proper authority?
Enforceability:	1. Is the **AGREEMENT** *prima facie* valid and enforceable? 2. Any obvious issue with enforcement of the Agreement?
Others material terms:	1. Is the Agreement subject to other material terms such as **RETENTION** of title clause, etc? If so, please state.

Recommendations (if any):	
Assumptions made:	If any assumptions have been made in preparing this report, please state:

Report updated as at:	[•]
Prepared by:	
Date:	

APPENDIX D: INDICATIVE OUTLINE FOR HORIZONTAL SCHEME OF MERGER

If you are in any doubt about the contents of this document or any action to be taken, you should consult your Stockbroker, Banker, Solicitor, Accountant or any other professional adviser duly registered under the investments and Securities Act No. 29, 2007 immediately.

If you have sold or otherwise transferred all your shares in Eureka Limited or Pegasus Plc please give this document and the accompanying proxy forms to the purchaser or transferee or to the Stockbroker, Bank or other agent through whom the sale or transfer was effected, for transmission to the purchaser or transferee.

The distribution of this document in jurisdictions other than Nigeria may be restricted by law and therefore persons into whose possession his document comes should inform themselves about and observe such restrictions. Any failure to comply with such restrictions may constitute a violation of the securities laws of such jurisdiction.

SCHEME OF MERGER

(PURSUANT TO PART XII OF THE INVESTMENT AND SECURITIES ACT NO. 29 2007)

BETWEEN

EUREKA LIMITED (Regn. No. ....)

AND

PEGASUS (Regn. No. ....)

Incorporating an Explanatory Statement on the Proposed Scheme of Merger

Capital Plc (regulated by the Securities & Exchange Commission) is acting as Financial Adviser of Pegasus Plc and Finance Service Limited (also regulated by the Securities & Exchange Commission) is acting as Financial Adviser to Eureka Limited.

Capital Plc will not be responsible to any person, individual or corporate body other than Pegasus Plc in relation to the transactions and arrangements referred to herein.

Finance Service Limited will not be responsible to any person, individual or corporate body other than Eureka Limited in relation to the transactions and arrangements referred to herein.

Notices convening the respective Court-Ordered Meetings of Pegasus Plc and Eureka Limited are set out on pages 101 to 108. To be valid, proxy forms must be completed, signed and stamped (together with the Power of Attorney or other authority- if any-under which they are signed and in accordance with the instructions printed thereon), and must be returned to the respective Registrars of Pegasus Plc and Eureka Limited as the case may be, not later than 24 hours before the time scheduled for the respective Court-Ordered Meetings.

THE PROPOSALS, WHICH ARE THE SUBJECT OF THE SCHEME FOR THE PROPOSED MERGER SET OUT IN THIS DOCUMENT, HAVE BEEN CLEARED WITH THE SECURITIES & EXCHANGE COMMISSION, THE ACTIONS THAT YOU ARE REQUESTED TO TAKE ARE SET OUT ON PAGES 20 OF THIS SCHEME DOCUMENT, NOTICES OF THE COURT ORDERED MEETINGS TO BE HELD ARE SET OUT ON PAGES 101 TO 108.

FINANCIAL ADVISER TO PEGASUS PLC FINANCIAL ADVISER TO EUREKA LIMITED

THIS SCHEME OF MERGER DOCUMENT IS DATED SEPTEMBER ….., 2013

www.ingramcontent.com/pod-product-compliance
Lightning Source LLC
Chambersburg PA
CBHW071349230926
51846CB00002B/489
* 9 7 8 9 4 0 3 5 3 0 2 1 5 *